Sunshine
for the
Latter-day Saint Teenager's Soul

Sunshine
for the
Latter-day Saint Teenager's Soul

BOOKCRAFT
Salt Lake City, Utah

Library of Congress Catalog Card Number: 99-73151

ISBN: 1-57008-659-1

Printed in the United States of America   72082-4888A

10   9   8   7   6   5   4   3

Contents

Friendship and Dating

Faith and Prayer

Attitude and Self-Worth

Choices

Testimony and Missionary Work

Family

Work and Goals

$\mathcal{P}$reface

You're a Latter-day Saint teenager, and that means you have some wonderful opportunities—along with some important responsibilities. President Gordon B. Hinckley has said to the youth of the Church: "Never forget that you were chosen and brought to earth as a child of God for something of importance in His grand design. He expects marvelous things of you. He expects you to keep your lives clean from the sins of the world" (*Teachings of Gordon B. Hinckley* [Salt Lake City: Deseret Book Co., 1997], p. 712).

There is great motivating power in realizing that such expectations apply to you. It can inspire you and give you the determination to live according to gospel principles. At times, however, you may find that living up to those expectations seems difficult. Obstacles and distractions try to trip you up and divert you away from the path of righteousness.

Well, it might help you to know that there are many people who understand what you're going through, who are rooting for you, who are calling out words of encouragement.

And that's what *Sunshine for the Latter-day Saint Teenager's Soul* is all about. This collection of stories and poems brings together words of wit, wisdom, and warning from several outstanding authors, and it is designed to give you a lift, a boost, a friendly push in the right direction. It is hoped that you will come away from these stories feeling motivated and strengthened in your resolve to be the best Latter-day Saint you can be.

One of the appealing things about this book is that you don't have to read it cover to cover (although you may decide to do just that!). You can pick and choose the stories that sound most interesting to you and read them in any order you want. The selections are arranged under such topics as service, friendship, prayer, self-worth, choices, testimony, family, and goals, and so there's bound to be *something* among all of these offerings that you will find enjoyable, helpful, or inspiring.

So read on, and let some sunshine into your soul. Then perhaps your heart and your mind will be all the more receptive to President Hinckley's admonition: "Believe in yourselves, in your capacity to do things that are good and worthwhile and upstanding" (*Teachings of Gordon B. Hinckley,* p. 715).

Bookcraft expresses gratitude to the authors whose works make up this volume. (Readers will note that virtually all of the selections are from Latter-day Saint authors, the exception being some wonderful poems by Edgar A. Guest, with whose sentiments Latter-day Saints so often find themselves in harmony.) The publisher also extends thanks to Maureen Mills, Lori Stevens, Lisa Valdivieso, Brooke Steed, and Lesley Taylor for their help in selecting, compiling, and arranging the 101 stories and poems included in this book.

Youth
of
Zion

Curses, Foiled Again

CHRIS CROWE

Walt was the new kid at school that year. He wasn't in any of my classes; I met him at our first freshman football practice. He seemed like a decent enough guy—a little on the quiet side, though.

I was the exact opposite—in the worst way. I wasn't LDS and talked long and loud with generous helpings of cussing. But despite our differences, I put up with Walt because he was such a good athlete. When it came to playing football, Walt was definitely all action and no talk.

I guess Walt had only two problems fitting in with the rest of us: he was the only Mormon on the team, and he was also the only kid who never, ever swore.

By the end of our freshman year, though, everybody was used to Walt and his quiet, cussless ways. Even though he looked like us and hung around with us, when he opened his mouth— or didn't open his mouth—he was completely different from us.

Walt's "sissy" vocabulary didn't bother me much the first couple of years I knew him. We became pretty good buddies and spent lots of time together talking about football, girls, school, and religion—Walt was always talking about his church. Anyway, in all our times together I never heard Walt swear, even when I figured he had every reason to.

At the beginning of our junior year I decided it was my duty to reform Walt by "improving" his vocabulary. It was our first year on the varsity—he was a defensive back, I was an offensive lineman—and I figured if he didn't learn to cuss he'd never fit in with the rest of the varsity squad.

"Look, Wally," I told him one night after practice (we were right in the middle of two-a-days), "I'm gonna make you swear—just once—if it's the last thing I do this year."

"Well," he grinned, "I guess that'll be the last thing you'll do, because I don't swear."

I had my work cut out for me. I mean, here was a guy who said "excuse me" every time he burped—even in the locker room. It was hard to believe that Walt didn't swear; he surely had plenty of cussing examples around him. The air in the locker room and football field was always filled with vivid streaks of blue language. I knew that he had heard everything there was to hear, but he still never used anything stronger than "Good grief," "darn," or "golly."

So I had to start at the beginning. One afternoon before practice I handed Walt a vocabulary list. "This is a list of words I want you to use today at practice. If you use them often enough, you'll finally get the hang of it, and before you know it, you'll be cussing like an old pro."

He looked over my list for a minute but didn't say a word.

I pointed to the first word. "This one—this is a great one. Use it when you drop an interception or miss a tackle. You'll really feel much better if you do. And the next few are good when somebody takes a cheap shot at you. Use these last two anytime the ref makes a bad call."

Walt wadded up my list and tossed it into his locker.

"Aw, c'mon, Wally," I pleaded. "Give it a chance. You've got to release all those pent-up emotions. You keep holding in all that anger and cussing and you'll have major ulcers before you're eighteen."

Out at practice that afternoon, Walt dropped an interception, missed three tackles during a scrimmage, and was the victim of one of my "friendly" cheap shots. I hit him right in the back, and when I helped him up, expecting to hear him cut loose with one of his new words, all he muttered was a feisty "Darn!"

I realized I needed more help if I was to reform Walt, so I recruited a few other guys to work on him. We tried everything:

booby-trapped his locker, pinched him in pileups, snapped him with towels, but we were lucky to get even a "doggone it" out of him. As a matter of fact, the harder we tried, the worse Walt got. It finally got so bad that he even quit using "darn" and just responded with "ouch" to all our persecutions.

"Okay, Walt," I said to him as we sat lacing up our cleats one day before practice, "I guess you win. No swearing, right? But what about dirty jokes? You know any?"

"Oh, you bet I do," he grinned. "I'll even tell you one today after practice."

After wind sprints that evening, before he even got off the field, I gathered our buddies around and announced, "Hey, you guys, listen to this. Walt's got a dirty joke to tell us."

"Yeah, right," said one player. "Walt? A dirty joke? You gotta be kidding."

"He wouldn't know a dirty joke if he heard one," said another. "This I gotta hear."

We huddled around Walt, anxious to see the effects of our reform efforts. "Gosh, you guys," he exclaimed, "give me some room, okay?" We all moved back. "All right." He blushed slightly. "This is it, my dirty joke: a white horse fell into a mud puddle."

"Oh no!" we moaned. "You call *that* a dirty joke?"

"Well, what'd you guys expect?" laughed Walt. "That's a *Mormon* dirty joke," he said as he trotted off to the locker room.

The football season progressed and so did Walt. He terrorized our opponents as much as he mystified us, so we dubbed him "the Stormin' Mormon." It was a well-deserved nickname.

It became a team obsession to pollute Walt, to make him more like us. We weren't vicious about it; we were just good-naturedly hoping to save him from going off the deep end of goody-goodness. As his teammates, we owed it to him. Unfortunately for us, he was just as good-natured and just as determined to remain in the deep end of goodness.

We weren't making any progress with Walt's vocabulary, so some guys began telling (that is, *trying* to tell) dirty jokes to him. As soon as they'd begin a story, he'd cover up his ears. If they increased their volume, Walt would sing out loud; the louder the story, the louder Walt sang.

It got to be pretty comical. Two guys would dance around Walt trying to tell him a dirty joke while he sat peacefully in front of his locker with both hands clapped flat over his ears, singing at the top of his lungs.

By the end of the season we'd all but given up on Walt. He was a lost cause as far as swearing went. There was simply no reforming him.

It was even worse our senior year. The younger players looked up to Walt because he was one of the top players on the team, and the rest of us knew there was no changing him, so we all just accepted him for what he was and left it at that. Of course, we didn't leave him *completely* alone. There were still a few booby-trapped lockers and assorted pranks. We gave Walt every opportunity, but he never swore.

And you know, we would have been disappointed if he had.

Things finally got so bad that even I started to give up cussing, especially around Walt. I knew he didn't like hearing profanity all the time, so I toned down my vocabulary.

After all we'd been through (and Walt had been through a lot more than I had), we were really good friends. We talked often about lots of things, and he continued to plug the Church every chance he got.

It's kind of funny, but for four years I was really trying, trying hard, to reform Walt—to help him see the light of using a man's vocabulary. But my bad example, and his good one, eventually backfired on me.

A month after we graduated, Walt was there to witness my baptism. "Gee whiz," he said after the ceremony, "I didn't think you'd ever change."

"Doggone it, Walt," I replied, "I'm glad *you* didn't."

On the Front Lines

KATHRYN SCHLENDORF

In struggling through medical school a young friend of mine had some bad days. You know the kind: the tests had all the wrong questions on them; he felt he was the only one who didn't get what the doctors were trying to teach him; his girlfriend decided to go on a mission just as he was planning to propose.

I got a phone call late one evening. "Kathy, I just don't understand. I go to church; I read my scriptures; I pay my tithing; I am trying to be good! Why won't Satan just leave me alone?"

I smiled inside, thinking that possibly those right choices might have something to do with it. "You need a blessing," I suggested, and recommended that he seek one.

He confided to me later what had happened when he went to the Lord for understanding. As a priesthood leader laid his hands on my friend's head, he learned at least part of why he was being tried so continuously: "In the War in Heaven you fought on the front lines with the archangel Michael against the forces of Satan, and you did not give an inch. He wants you now!"

My friend came out of that blessing with his chest about four inches thicker. "Just come on," he challenged, again ready for the fight.

Liquid Darkness

RAND PACKER

By the time I was fourteen years old I had been offered several opportunities to drink. This was not the "living waters" kind of drink, mind you, but more of the dying kind, the killing kind of waters that rob mankind of earthly and heavenly inheritance. Liquor is a cheater, a liar, and a thief. It mocks, mangles, and murders with a smile on its malicious face. Not only does it amputate sound judgment from the mind, but it transfuses the entire body with a dulling, numbing narcotic, causing an illusion of roses from nothing but rubbish.

The invitation to drink of liquid darkness is offered to people millions of times daily throughout the world and has been for ages. It has probably ruined more lives, destroyed more families, and caused more sin than any one commodity this world has ever known. Most everyone who lives in this world will have an encounter with it. It seeks out everyone, and either by force or by agency presents itself in a variety of costumes. The following story is my encounter with it. The incident took place when I was with a friend, and the memory of it has saved my life many times since.

If people could choose a year of life to skip, age fourteen would probably get the most votes. There is not a whole lot of good that happens to a young person at age fourteen, mainly because a lot of *bad* things seem to happen around that age. I have sometimes thought that when the youth reach age fourteen Satan unleashes his legions double-time because he is still mad that the Prophet Joseph Smith, at age fourteen, split the heavens through prayer and the First Vision occurred. Regardless of the reason, it is a tough and crucial time of life during which important decisions are made. Should I follow Satan, with all of his attractions? Or should I follow the Lord, with all of his meetings? At fourteen I found myself making such decisions with a quorum of other young men in the back of an old open-bed fire truck as we headed for the arid mountains of Utah's west desert.

"Rand, throw me that bag, wouldja?" one of the boys said.

"Sure thing, Dil," I responded, throwing his knapsack the length of the truck. "Dil" was the shortened version of this boy's nickname, "Diller." I'm not sure why we christened him with that name and what it really meant, but the name Diller fit him perfectly.

"I've gotta get some real food," he grinned with delight as our truck pulled into the last gas-and-goodies store before we started our ascent up the mountain. As was customary, we always stopped at a convenience store to supplement the carrots, apples, milk, and other health foods our mothers had packed for us. We preferred the more palatable, nutrition-less, and chemically preserved junk sweets that were free from all vitamins.

Following our food-replacement project, we commenced our hour-long drive to Mercur, onetime mining mecca of Utah but now a home for only ghosts and tumbleweeds. We were going to camp and eat and tell ghost stories and drop boulders down mine shafts and maybe sleep for ten minutes. We were fifteen yelling and hollering boys throwing stuff—free of walls and civilization and Mom and Dad.

Then it happened. A friend, turned enemy for the moment by the adversary, reached down into his pack and pulled out a can of liquid darkness. Everyone in the truck went awestruck silent as he popped the lid and held it high towards the sky. "If any of you are men," he bellowed above the roar of the diesel engine, "you'll have a drink with me!" The can quickly went to his lips as he drew a large swallow from the off-yellow can. He exhaled with gusto and passed it to the boy next to him.

All eyes were now on the can as the second boy received it into his waiting hand. I didn't think he would hesitate, and he performed true to my anticipation. In an instant the can was to his lips as he took a swig with great bravado in front of us all. The can moved to the next boy around the circle.

As the can moved my direction, my mind sprinted in search of some quick answer, some cool response that would rescue me from this dark pit I found myself in. I knew what was right and wrong. I knew what the Word of Wisdom said. I knew the story of the young boy Joseph and his infected leg and how the doctor suggested he be bound with cords to withstand the pain of frontier surgery. I knew the boy prophet's answer to that suggestion and also the next one that followed. "No, I will not touch one particle of liquor, neither will I be tied down." No liquor was to touch his lips, but he would let his father hold him in his arms. I remembered his pain-filled response to his blessed mother when she rushed in to calm his relentless cries as the physician broke off large pieces of infected bone. "Oh, Mother, go back, go back. I do not want you to come in. I will try to tough it out, if you will go away." They were the cries of a sober young man who, at age seven, was more man than most men. He was not filled with a numbing stupor but with pain and purifying obedience.

These things were racing in my mind as the can found its way to the third boy, a mousy little guy on his very first camp out. He had not come to break covenant or to be tempted. He thought he was going on a camp out. As he held the can I could sense the frantic search going on in his own mind to wake up from this terrible nightmare. All eyes were upon him, staring, forcing, demanding he drink as the others had. I could almost hear his pleading cries for his mother to come and save him, but she was nowhere to be found. He closed his eyes, nervously brought the can to his mouth, and let some darkness trickle down his throat. Try as he did, he could not handle the pressure. His countenance writhed in despair and the agony of sin. He hurriedly passed it to my friend, my buddy, my example, Richard Ambrose Call II.

Rick, I said to myself, *if you take one sip of that I'm going to slug you so hard.* My heart was pounding with the realization that I was next around the circle to receive the can, and my mind was absolutely empty as to how I was going to wiggle out of this one gracefully. I just knew that if I didn't take a drink, they would bury me up to my neck in the blue hills of Mercur and let the ants play tag through my nose and out my ears. And then it came. From somewhere deep inside "the city where God dwells," it came.

Rick held that yellow can out in front of us. He looked over at me; I looked over at him. We both looked up at the can he was holding. Then we looked up at the thirteen gawking faces waiting anxiously for the kill. Like wolves they were, fangs showing as they made themselves ready to pounce.

Rick looked over at me again. I looked over at him. We both looked up at the can. For a long moment he just stared at it, and then very casually he took the can of beer and put it down between his knees. He reached down into his pack, fished around for a minute until he found something, and then pulled it out. Like a small rock brought out of the pouch of David to be placed in his giant-killing sling, it came. It was the most beautiful purple thing I had ever seen. He raised it to heaven where all could see.

"If *any* of you are men," Rick yelled above the whine of the diesel engine, "you'll have a drink of grape soda with me!"

Rick popped the lid on the can, brought it to his lips with authority, swooned as that purple pop oozed down his thirsty throat, and passed it back the other direction.

I never got a drink from either can. The kid on the other side of Rick found himself holding a purple can now. He looked up and caught the stare of the wolves. He couldn't handle the pressure. He just had to take a drink of that grape soda. He quickly did so and passed it to the boy on the other side of him. As they were enjoying the pressure of purple purge, Rick reached down between his knees, grabbed the can of yucky yellow, and heaved it over the side of the truck. I shall never forget seeing that can, frothing at one end as it turned in the air, descend into the gully below.

It just takes one person, one person who is willing to stand in a world of darkness and show forth a little light. The light is not his or hers, mind you. Its source is the great Elohim and his Beloved Son. Just as surely as a single lightbulb can illuminate the darkest of rooms, so can a single individual chase away the engulfing darkness of the opponents of heaven.

God bless you, Richard Ambrose Call II, for the light you turned on in the back of an old open-bed fire truck on a dark and winding road in the mountains of Mercur.

At the Top

JOHN A. GREEN

There were twenty-seven of us that day, all eighteen or nineteen years of age, except one fellow, twenty-one, whom we called "Pop." Three more had started out with us in our flight but had washed out along the way, unable to keep up with the grueling physical discipline of basic training in the Royal Canadian Air Force. We had been training hard for months to take the place of young men not much older than ourselves who, at watch behind machine guns and Plexiglas bubbles, were still giving their lives over Germany.

Traditionally, completion of basic training called for a fitting "graduation ceremony." Each flight was confident that it could outperform any other group in almost any sort of physical contest. The flight party at the end of basic training had become the recognized way for flight trainees to prove that they were second to none.

Our flight was no different. A youthful eagerness seemed to be pushing us to throw off the discipline for a night, to noisily proclaim that we were the top, and to somehow cram into one furious evening enough pleasure to last a lifetime. And so twenty-seven of us sat down on the grass that day to discuss our flight party.

I sat down feeling very alone, and for the first time since our flight had been formed, I felt absolutely no desire to be part of the group. I watched the others smiling and laughing as they agreed that only a top nightclub would do, and I sensed the mounting excitement as they discussed the activities that they felt would be the most entertaining. It was suggested that each of us had an obligation to contribute his best thoughts on the matter, and after five or six fellows had enthusiastically expressed their ideas, someone said, "Let's hear what Green has to say."

Green was the only Mormon in the group and had no desire to say anything to anybody. All he wanted to do was withdraw. How do you tell twenty-six non-Mormons about the branch you attend every Sunday with a fellow Mormon from another flight? How do you convey the feelings you have about the mission home where you have a standing invitation every Sunday for dinner, and where you gather around the piano every Sunday evening to sing with the missionaries just before you and your buddy leave to catch the last streetcar back to the barracks before lights out? What could you say to twenty-six non-Mormons planning an all-out bash in a nightclub about how cold and dismal that Sunday night ride back to the barracks seemed? How sensitive would they be to your observation that you loathed setting foot in the barracks every Sunday night because you knew that the first word you heard would make a complete mockery of the word *love?*

The answer to all those questions, as they passed quickly through my mind that day, was: "They wouldn't understand. They wouldn't care. They'd probably sneer or laugh. Their idea of a flight party is a good indication of what they find important in life, and therefore it's pointless to talk to them." But somehow I had to come up with something that would get me off the hook, that would let me withdraw from the flight party. I was angry with myself because, after months of working together as a team with these fellows, I was going to suddenly and painfully resign. I was angry at them for putting me in a situation that I knew I was going to mishandle. They were going to judge me as the last type of person they wanted at the flight party, and I had already judged them as incapable of organizing a party I would want to attend.

"Let's hear what Green has to say."

"Yeah, Green. You haven't said a word. What do you want to do?"

Green drew a deep breath and, looking rather sullenly at the grass in front of him, made his brief withdrawal speech: "Well, if I were to go to a flight party . . . I'd be taking a pretty decent girl . . . so there'd be no drinking . . . and no smoking . . . and no swearing." He didn't dare look at anyone, and he gathered himself as best he could against the sudden onslaught he knew was coming.

And then it happened.

There was a good minute of utter silence. It was so still you could have heard a pin drop on the grass. Then someone from across the circle began to speak:

"Well . . ."

This was it. This was going to be the start. They would all have their say, and then Green could beat his solitary retreat, leaving his worldly buddies with their frivolous taste for life.

"Well . . . I'd be taking a pretty nice girl myself . . ."

From beside him, "Who wouldn't?"

There was another good minute of silence, and then, from off to the right, "I nominate Green as master of ceremonies." There were no other nominations.

A week later, all twenty-seven members of the flight brought their beautifully dressed dates to our party. There was no drinking, no smoking, no swearing. Just lots of good food, good music, good dancing . . . and good memories of a flight party that was rather unique.

I remember, not without embarrassment, my thoughts on that sunny afternoon in 1944 as we sat down together on the grass. I remember that, unintentionally, I touched the lives of twenty-six young men. I thought I was putting them down. Generously, they put me at the top, and in my memory that's exactly where I see them.

Holding the Standard

ARDETH G. KAPP

Shelly was not quite sixteen when a young man invited her to a school dance. It's hard to hold the standard sometimes, especially when it seems that all your friends are going. Shelly tried to explain the standard of not dating until you're sixteen. "It was really hard," she said, "especially when you don't understand yourself that even though you are almost sixteen, you have to wait. Sometimes it just doesn't make sense. I guess it's just a matter of obedience. After struggling to say no when I wanted to say yes, I felt terrible. It hurt, until my friend who had invited me left the following note in my locker: 'Hi, Shelly. I think you're great. Through all the times I have been privileged to be with you, I have never failed to be impressed. You are one of the very few people who live exactly the way they profess to live. That is unique, an exceptional accomplishment. You have so many gifts and have learned to use them wisely. Your spirit is full of life and giving. You are so willing to share. You bless all who know you; no wonder so many people watch and follow your example. God bless you, Shelly.' "

Shelly survived that hard time, and the following year she had many dates and many friends, both members and nonmembers.

$\mathscr{A}$ Dollar Too Much

KATHRYN SCHLENDORF

A young Latter-day Saint was a successful athlete in a small-town high school. He was a good kid and a good competitor, but no matter how well he performed, his coach constantly chided him because he was "straight"—because he didn't participate in the typical after-game activities of the other guys. His language was different, his attitude was different, and the coach noticed the separation, and commented on it constantly. It couldn't have been any worse if the coach had publicly exclaimed, "What do you do after our games—go home and play Barbies with your sister?"

The sarcastic jibes seemed to continue without let up, so that the boy dreaded any encounter with his coach.

It was under these circumstances that, at the conclusion of the high school football season, he went to turn in his equipment and uniform and collect his deposit money. The coach gave him the money, but as it turned out, the young man was given too much. A dollar too much.

"Oh great," he thought to himself. The idea of approaching his coach about the matter was not appealing. He could see it now—waving the dollar in the air and singing, "Here coach, I'm so honest. Here is the extra dollar you gave me!" No way. He wasn't about to set himself up for more ridicule. The coach had just lost a dollar.

The next morning came, and because of the kind of kid he was, the young athlete realized that he couldn't keep the money. He made his way as inconspicuously as he could to the coach's desk, and laid down the dollar bill.

17

"You gave me a dollar too much," he mumbled, and then tore for the door. He was an athlete, and he intended to use his speed to get out of there before the coach would have time to say too much.

As he ran away, he heard the coach bark out, "Pay up!" Startled, the boy stopped, and turned to see his coach standing with his open hand extended to his assistant coach.

What the young Latter-day Saint hadn't realized, but suddenly became aware of, was that he had been set up. He had been given back a dollar too much on purpose. And his gloating coach had bet his assistant *one hundred dollars* that the "Mormon kid" would bring the dollar back.

People *are* watching you. Can they bet on you?

$\mathscr{H}$er Future Children

CURTIS L. JACOBS

While my mother and father were serving their mission, they heard two Elders tell of teaching a young Jewish lady who was currently dating an LDS young man. In her journal my mother wrote: "He had just accepted a position over in Taiwan, where he had been a missionary. She felt that she must have the discussions to make up her mind about joining the Church and going with him. . . . They gave her one discussion and she said that she wanted them all the next day. So they were giving her the discussions, and afterwards she told them that as they were talking there was an 'aura' around them and she could see people looking at her from behind the missionaries; and she now asked who they were. The missionaries didn't have an answer, but went back to their apartment and prayed. . . . It was revealed to them . . . that they were her [future] children that would be born to her and this young man. They were waiting to see if she would accept the gospel. She did, and was baptized."

$\mathcal{T}$he Toast

CHRIS CROWE

Tom joined the Church in Germany. When he turned nineteen, he was required to join the army, where his new LDS standards were soon tested.

"As soldiers," he said, "we had to live in large barracks, and I couldn't avoid being in situations which conflicted with the teaching of the Church and the principles I had recently gained a testimony of.

"Some friends threw a party to celebrate my promotion to lieutenant. At such parties, it was the custom that a high-ranking officer give a talk, and after the talk everyone would drink a toast of champagne.

"Knowing this, I went to my commanding officer beforehand and told him that because I was LDS, I couldn't drink any alcohol. He told me that if I didn't drink the toast, it would be a serious breach of etiquette.

"I told him I was sorry, but I would not drink. My commanding officer couldn't understand why I wouldn't make an exception. I told him it was a commandment of God, and I couldn't break it. I asked him if he would break one of God's commandments if he knew the commandment truly was from God.

"He told me he would not. Then I bore him my testimony that I knew the Lord had commanded Mormons not to drink alcohol.

"At the party, everyone toasted with champagne except me. I had orange juice—orange juice provided by my commanding officer."

Service, Love, and Compassion

The Angel

MARK ELLISON

Let's get a move on, Elder!" I yelled at my lazy missionary companion. Fully dressed in my crisp, new navy blue suit, scriptures in hand, name tag in place, I was ready and eagerly waiting to venture forth from our humble little missionary apartment and preach repentance to the wicked world outside.

My slowpoke companion, however, was still shaving. I paced back and forth in our miniature living room. It was so small that you couldn't pace far. One or two steps in one direction, that was it; then you had to turn. Pace, pace, pace. I waited, then yelled again: "Come on, Elder Raymond!"

"Keep yer shirt on, El-durr!" he hollered back in his Ozark Mountain drawl.

That's my companion, I thought, as I resumed my pacing. *My lazy, ball-and-chain, sloth-of-a-missionary companion. Great! I get a burnt-out, trunky, about-to-go-home Elder for my first companion in the mission field.* I grew red with frustration. Mission rules said we had to be out of our apartment and busy at our missionary labors by nine-thirty each morning. I looked down at my watch. It was ten-forty-seven. I decided it was time to yell again. "It's no wonder we don't have any investigators to teach!"

"Hey!" Elder Raymond's mousey little face, half-covered with shaving cream, appeared in the bathroom doorway. "Put a lid on it, Ellison."

It's kind of funny now to look back on the difficulty I had in getting along with Elder Raymond, but at the time there was nothing funny about it. There I was, on my *mission,* the experience that was supposed to be the spiritual pinnacle of my life thus far, and I was having these terrible feelings of impatience and anger!

I had never even imagined that my mission would contain the possibility of such contention. But the lifestyle sure was challenging. I was never to leave the presence of my companion. The first thing I'd see in the morning and the last thing I'd see at night was his face. I'd hear his singing, listen to his dumb jokes and the stories about his family, eat his cooking, and see all his weaknesses. He and I seemed totally different: I was raised in the fast-paced subculture of southern California, and he was raised in the hillbilly lands of Missouri. I talked fast, he talked slow.

As the weeks went by, our missionary work seemed to drag. I mean, it was *slow*—I mean slower than cold molasses trying to drip uphill in January. We couldn't seem to find *anyone* interested in talking with us. As we encountered disappointment after disappointment I became convinced that it was all Elder Raymond's fault. *He* was the slow one. I began to miss home, family, girls, my truck, and my guitar. Soon I had developed a truly spectacular case of homesickness, and that too was his fault, I felt. I began to hate my companion. And guess what happened to the Spirit in our missionary work! It left. Now, that's no way for a missionary to live.

A terrible, dark feeling accompanies contention. It is the opposite of the love, peace, and joy which accompany the Spirit of the Lord. "The spirit of contention is not of me," said the Savior, "but is of the devil, who is the father of contention, and he stirreth up the hearts of men to contend with anger, one with another" (3 Nephi 11:29).

What should we do when we have a hard time getting along with someone? Elder Richard L. Evans used to say, "Anyone can get along with perfect people, but our task is to get along with imperfect people." I think the Lord understood that we would sometimes have difficulty in doing that. Nevertheless he instructed us, "Love your enemies." Now, how do you love someone you can't stand, or who can't stand you? Well, the Lord gave us some ideas as he further instructed us: "*Bless them* that curse you, *do good to them* that hate you, and *pray for them* which despitefully use you, and persecute you" (Matthew 5:44; emphasis added).

One morning, while Elder Raymond was showering, I sat on my bed reading the scriptures. Actually, I was reading *a* scripture, the same verse, over and over—not because it was especially inspiring, but because I couldn't concentrate; I had to keep thinking, *Where was I?* and start reading over again. I couldn't concentrate because out of the corner of my eye I could see Elder Raymond's messy bed. I knew it would take him forever to make his bed, get dressed, and be ready to go, and the very thought had me fuming. I yelled toward the bathroom, "Elder, how long are you going to be?" No answer.

Finally, I put my scriptures down, stomped over to my companion's bed, and made it for him—fluffed up the pillow, tucked in the sheets, the works. Then I sat back down on my bed and returned to my reading. I could finally concentrate.

A few minutes later a bathrobe-clad Elder Raymond walked in. He stood in the doorway, looking at the room, perplexed. I pretended not to notice. "Say, El-durr," he drawled, "di' joo make mah behhd?"

I decided to play innocent. "Why, no, Elder, but it looks really good. Just a sec—I'm almost done with this chapter—and then I'll join you for companion prayer."

"Now, hold on," Elder Raymond muttered, his brow furrowed in thought. "Ah know *Ah* didn't make mah behhd, and . . . thar's just yew and me here . . . *yew* must've made mah behhd!"

Well, now you know I was wrong when I said my companion was slow.

"No, really," I insisted. I was beginning to have fun with this. "It must have been someone else." Then I smiled. "Maybe an angel came down and did it."

That really cracked up Elder Raymond. "An angel, eh? Har, har, har!"

The next morning, as Elder Raymond showered, I quickly made his bed for him again—big, fluffy pillow; nice, tight hospital corners, the way my mom had taught me; I could have bounced a quarter three feet off the covers, no fooling. Then I sat on my bed, read my scriptures, and tried not to laugh. Moments later, in walked my companion. "Say, El-durr, joo make mah behhd agin?"

"It wasn't me, Elder, honest."

"Looks lahk that *angel* come back agin, eh?"

"Yeah, must've been The Angel."

Once again, this struck him as being absolutely hilarious. "Har, har, har, har!"

The Angel struck every morning for a week, and then one morning Elder Raymond said to me, with a half-suppressed grin, "Say, El-durr, why don't yew go shower first today?" I did, and as I came back into the bedroom a few minutes later I noticed that *my* bed had been made! The pillow was fluffed up, the sheets tucked in neatly. Elder Raymond sat on his bed, pretending to be engrossed in the scriptures. I smiled and asked, "Say, El-durr, *joo make mah behhd?*"

He laughed and said, "Musta been that *angel* agin!"

Well, from that time on Elder Raymond and I began to do nice things for each other, and we'd usually blame them on The Mysterious Elusive Angel. I discovered that my companion had a good sense of humor! We began to enjoy each other's company, and to sing together as we worked. It lifted our spirits and made our days happier. I no longer hated my companion. I *liked* him— really, truly, genuinely liked him. And I liked being a missionary again. And guess what happened to the Spirit in our companionship! It came back.

We began to have good experiences talking with people about the gospel. I learned many things from Elder Raymond about how to teach and converse with people. We saw some of our investigators enter the waters of baptism and make covenants with their Father in Heaven, and join the church of his Son, Jesus Christ. We shared many spiritual experiences.

I'll never forget the day when we knocked on the door of a lady who was in terrible pain with a back injury. We taught her about priesthood blessings. Elder Raymond and I laid our hands on her head and blessed her by the power of the Melchizedek Priesthood. The influence of the Spirit was powerful as my good companion boldly declared that this lady's pain would subside immediately. After the blessing, the lady stood with eyes wide and wondering, and quietly spoke: "My pain is gone." Elder Raymond and I testified that we were representatives of the church that held the power and authority of God, and the lady said, "Thank God for young men like you, who go about in the world doing good." And you know what? I began to love my companion. I loved Elder Raymond.

$\mathscr{A}$ Chance to Dance

SHANE BARKER

As a teacher I was supervising a school dance once when I saw Teresa, a girl from one of my classes. She was standing off to the side, all by herself. She wasn't an attractive girl, and she wasn't very popular. I knew that she wasn't going to dance much.

But I happened to know that she liked a boy named Mike. (She had his name written all over her folders.)

It also happened that Mike was a friend of mine, so I went up to him and said, "How'd you like to do me a favor?"

"Sure."

"There's a girl I'd like you to dance with. Would you ask her?"

My respect for Mike went up 100 percent. He didn't ask who she was; he simply said, "Sure."

I pointed her out. And my admiration for him went up another 100 percent. He didn't pull a face. And he didn't say, "Boy, you're gonna owe me big for this one." Instead, he just nodded.

"Okay," he said. "Do you want me to ask her right now?"

I shook my head. "No. Just sometime. I just think it would be cool if she got a chance to dance tonight."

"Okay," he said again. "I'll do it."

He did, too. I saw them as they walked onto the dance floor, and she was *glowing*.

But the classy thing about Mike was that he asked her *twice more*.

Mike lifted a life that night. With no thought for himself—and without worrying what anyone would think—he blessed Teresa's life.

Who Can I Make Happier Today?

RANDALL C. BIRD

I remember well a young lady from a seminary class I taught who approached me and asked, "Who can I make happier today? Have you seen anyone who needs a lift?"

I thought for a few minutes; then I gave her the name of a young man who could use some cheering up.

Well, I didn't need to say another word. For a solid week this young lady put nice notes, candy, and other "warm fuzzies" into this young man's locker. He didn't know who was being so kind to him; he only knew that he could hardly wait to visit his locker each day. He became a new person. He was happy about school, life, and his family. He talked more to others, and his confidence began to "wax strong" (D&C 121:45) because a girl's kindness led his thoughts toward the good things of life instead of gloom and darkness.

$\mathcal{A}$ Pick-Me-Up

STEPHEN JASON HALL

When I first left the hospital after a diving accident that left me paralyzed from the chest down, I badly wanted to reenter high school. I knew that my weak body and decreased stamina would not allow me to return full-time, so I would only be able to attend a few classes. At the same time, I had physical therapy to attend from morning until early afternoon. This meant that if I was to attend school I would have to go to early-morning classes, then go to therapy, and then return to school for the final hour of the day.

When I started back to school, my mother did all the driving. She was always glad to do it, and she worked hard to balance her schedule at home to make it work. But it began to take its toll on her and on my younger brothers and sister. After a few months, two of my close friends, Scott and Susie, noticed the effort it took on my mother's part and the difficulty it caused for my family, so they offered to pick me up and drop me off at home each day. This task was not as simple or easy as it sounds. They would have to get up early (sometimes only to wait for me), lift me in and out of the car, and make sure my clothes looked just right and my school supplies were all situated correctly—only to repeat the whole process at the end of the day.

This was not easy or convenient for them. They stood to gain nothing from completing the task. Yet they did it, not only driving me to school but to activities, study groups, church affairs, and even once to toilet-paper our teacher's yard. They never complained or made me feel as though I was a burden. They were always cheerful and happy to do it. When they would come and pick me up for school, they picked up not only my body but my spirit as well. I was included. They made me feel that I was just another member of a car pool.

They were willing to sacrifice for me daily because they were truly my friends. For being a friend means active participation in the journey of life. And as we drive onward we must work to do all we can to be like Susie and Scott. We must seek out spirits to pick up and carry along. Often we think we know who our friends are, and what it means to be a friend, but when sacrifice is necessary, we truly know.

"You're Going to L.A."

RANDAL A. WRIGHT

Years ago I taught early-morning seminary in southeast Texas. It was not easy having a full-time job, serving on the stake high council, and teaching five mornings a week starting at 5:55 A.M. Some of you will have that assignment in the future. There were several mornings when I was not prepared as well as I should have been. There were times when I was afraid to stand in front of the class. But those seminary students accepted me as I was and became my friends.

On one occasion, I mentioned that my cousin Ned was getting married in the Los Angeles Temple. Knowing that Ned had been my good friend growing up, someone asked if I was going to his wedding. I replied that I would love to go, but I had to give a talk and sing that weekend and I couldn't afford it anyway. Several weeks later, I walked into the classroom and the students wanted me to play a game. I went throughout the building looking for clues they'd hidden. Back in our classroom, I was instructed to pull the curtains back and read what was written on the chalkboard. I didn't fully grasp the meaning of the message at first. It said:

> Put on your rags,
> And shine your shoes.
> Grab your bags.
> We've got good news.
>
> We canceled your talk
> And also your song.

You're going to L.A.—
But not for too long.

You need to go home
So you can get ready,
For later this evening
You will see Neddie!

We love you!
The Seniors of '85

Taped to the board was an envelope that the students encouraged me to open. Inside I found two plane tickets to L.A. These students had saved their money (including lunch money) to buy me a ticket to attend my cousin's wedding. I will never forget the love shown. They overlooked the days I had come to class unprepared; they loved me and sacrificed for me despite my faults. They truly followed the Savior's admonition, "This is my commandment, That ye love one another, as I have loved you" (John 15:12).

Nobody Is Not Your Name

GARY R. NELSON

In my years of instructing students in seminary and youth groups I have come across dozens of young people searching for an identity, youth who believed they were Nobodies. Somehow through the love of God and his Spirit they could feel that "he denieth none that come unto him . . . and all are alike unto God" (2 Nephi 26:33), that God would touch their lives through someone else, to help them believe that they were in fact a Somebody. In the words of the Lord to the prophet Samuel we read, "Look not on his countenance, or on the height of his stature . . . for the Lord seeth not as man seeth; for man looketh on the outward appearance, but the Lord looketh on the heart" (1 Samuel 16:7).

Such was the case with a student named Darrel. He was a sophomore at Roy High School, located near Ogden in northern Utah. Darrel needed and demanded a lot of attention. Like a puppy dog, he followed me everywhere I went. During lunch and before and after school, he appeared. He just wanted to be listened to, reckoned with, needed, accepted . . . loved! He had been told all of his nearly fifteen years of life that he was a Nobody, and he was believing this deceptive lie. Something within me whispered that he had a higher destiny. I felt that the only positive strokes he received all day came from me. I tried to take and make time for Darrel, even though at times it was difficult. He so badly wanted to be accepted that he would do almost anything for attention or to be noticed in my class. He would offer to say the prayer, read the scriptures or the story, or volunteer to be the first to want to be a part of the object lesson or role-play experience. One day my class was in one of those

"We're too cool to do anything spiritual today" moods. Darrel wanted to be involved. So I involved him. He ended up doing everything on the devotional! He led the music, said the prayer, read the scripture, and did the object lesson.

One day Darrel came up to me and said, "Guess what, Brother Nelson! Tomorrow is my fifteenth birthday! I just thought you'd like to know!" I had a pair of "sunshine officers" who were chosen as class officers. They anonymously went around doing things for people in the class; they would recognize birthdays and other special events in the lives of their classmates. I asked both Lori and Sheila to please put together a cake and a thoughtful card that we could give to Darrel the next day.

Bless their hearts, Sheila and Lori came through! But Darrel did not show up to class the next day. After some follow-up calls with the school I found out he had checked out of school and moved over to Clearfield that day. We could have dropped the opportunity to serve, but we did not—we felt impressed to find him. With Darrel's new address in hand and both class officers in the back of my car, we headed for Clearfield after school. We found that Darrel lived in a trailer court located in a poorer section of the city. As we entered the trailer park and started hitting the first of many speed-control bumps, there stood Darrel straddling his Sting Ray bicycle. The bike had no chain, and both tires were flat. He was having a good time just pushing it around. He shuffled over to us and said, "Brother Nelson! You remembered my birthday. *You remembered my birthday!*" He motioned to have us follow him and led us to a shabby, aluminum-clad trailer.

He invited us inside to meet his parents. Lori and Sheila followed with the surprise chocolate cake and candles hidden behind their backs. His parents were gracious, yet backward in appearance and dress. Even though their vocabulary was simple, their manners were genuine and appreciative. "Mom and Dad," Darrel said, "this is Brother Nelson, my seminary teacher. He's come here along with Sheila and Lori to wish me a happy birthday." We withdrew from behind our backs the surprise cake and lit the fifteen candles. We sang him "Happy Birthday," and the parents joined in. It was a thrill to watch him blow all the candles out. Tears streamed down his face, and we too were touched by the spirit of this moment. As he choked back the tears, he motioned us to follow him out of the door. We said our good-byes and walked down the trailer-house steps. He threw his arms around my neck and exclaimed, "Thanks, Brother Nelson, for coming. You know, this is the *first* birthday cake I have ever received in my life. Thanks so much!" Tears filled our own eyes. He gave us his official bicycle escort out of the trailer court. We left spiritually lifted and subdued.

Each of us has felt like a Nobody at some time. We have all felt like failures; we have all had those feelings of discouragement that come with low self-esteem and lack of appreciation and attention. But I can testify that each of you young people is somebody, somebody really special. I know that God loves you. You were divinely created and should be divinely motivated to look at your differences in a positive and not a negative way. You possess greatness and have bright futures. In your quest for knowledge and understanding about yourself, please always remember that you are somebody, and Nobody is not your name.

*W*hat Would Jesus Do—and Why?

MICHAEL WEIR ALLRED

Have you ever been told to ask yourself, "What would Jesus do?" I think this is great advice, but I would like to add one more part.

When I was ten to twelve years old my little nephew had been hurt and his mother thought he had a concussion. She called my mother and asked us to go get them and take them to the hospital. While we were at their house, my mother went inside with my sister and my nephew and left me alone in the car.

What would Jesus do? I loved this nephew very much and didn't want him to be hurt. So I knelt down on the floor and prayed to my Heavenly Father that he wouldn't have a concussion. He was too little: if someone should have to have a concussion, it should be me. Is that what Jesus would do?

When we arrived at the hospital, to our joy my nephew did not have a concussion. The Lord had answered my prayer. In fact, he answered it in every detail, because not long after that I fell in a shower and got a concussion. If I were to say that same prayer today, I would leave out that little part about *my* getting the concussion.

Not only should we ask what Jesus would do but we should also ask why. Why would the Savior go to church? Why would the Savior obey the Word of Wisdom? Why would the Savior study the scriptures every day? There are three main reasons why people do good: fear, pride, and love. The Savior's motivation is always love. When we begin to do *right,* we are going in the *right* direction. When we begin to do the *right* things for the *right* reasons, then we are *right*eous.

In the general conference of October 1986 Elder Neal A. Maxwell said, "We cannot share in His power without sharing in His attributes. . . . We cannot reenter His house until our behavior would let us feel at home" (" 'God Will Yet Reveal,' " *Ensign,* November 1986, p. 54). When it is time for us to come home, will the Father know his child?

"*My* Choice Is You!"

MARK A. BYBEE

Kirk knocked on the door of the room where I was teaching a seminary class and asked if he could come in and ask a girl to one of the main dances at the school. Kirk was a state champion wrestler, a football player, and a handsome, popular athlete with whom any girl would love to have a date.

As Kirk wandered around the room—back and forth, up and down the aisle, with roses in his hand—he recited a poem of love and caring and a desire to take a particular girl to the dance. Every girl watched with anticipation as he strolled towards her, and then with a forlorn expression as he passed her by.

The most bright-eyed girl in the room was Becky, not because of anticipation on her own behalf but because of her love for life, her caring for all the other girls in the class, and her excitement for these types of curious activities in the classroom. Anticipation for herself was the furthest thing from her mind—she had been confined to a wheelchair for many years because of a long-term disease. Her eyes glistened and her smile broadened as Kirk continued to pace around the room and recite his poem. The entire class broke into a sigh followed by tears from every eye as Kirk placed the flowers on Becky's desk and proclaimed: "And my choice is you! Will you go with me?"

Becky's emotions would not allow her to answer at that time, so Kirk just asked her to think about it and then left. It is my understanding that the date was a complete success. Kirk took her out on the floor in her wheelchair and danced all around her as she danced within her chair. On the last dance of the evening he picked her up out of the chair and danced all around the dance floor with her cradled in his arms as she laughed and cried. I'll never forget her expression on the last day of class as we had a small testimony meeting. There Becky expressed thanks for that experience and said she could hardly wait for the resurrection, when she would be able to "dance and dance and dance."

Christmas Package

SHANE BARKER

I went to the post office one afternoon in December. An elderly man there was trying to mail a Christmas package to his grandson, who was a missionary in England. But he didn't have enough money to send it airmail.

"How long will it take to go by boat?" he asked.

The clerk shrugged. "A month . . . maybe six weeks."

The old man's shoulders slumped. It wouldn't get there in time for Christmas.

Just then, a clerk at the opposite end of the counter called, "Next!"

I stepped up to the window.

"What can I do for you?" he asked.

"I've got a couple of things to send," I said. "But I need you to do me a favor first."

"Sure. What do you need?"

"There's a man at the end of the counter sending a package to England. I'd like to pay for it. And I'd like to send it airmail."

The clerk nodded and started to walk away.

"Just a second," I said. "You can't tell him who's paying for it."

He nodded, then walked down the aisle, where he whispered to the other clerk. When he returned he asked, "Is that your grandfather?"

I shook my head. "No. I've never met him."

"That was nice of you."

I was embarrassed. "It's Christmas," I said.

That particular Christmas I was a little short of money myself. But I felt like a million dollars as I drove home.

Halloween Santa

ELAINE CANNON

A small girl dressed up in her Halloween costume as a Salvation Army Santa Claus, complete with the relentless tingle-tingle of a bell on a long black handle, and went her way for treats. Her bag was full when she knocked at one last door. The lady of the house said she was sorry but her store of goodies was empty—every last treat had been handed out.

The young Santa began ringing her bell merrily and said, "That's okay. I have plenty. I'll give you some of mine!"

It has indeed been said, "A little child shall lead them."

$\mathcal{H}$e Knew What Team He Was On

KATHRYN SCHLENDORF

$\mathbf{M}$y first off-campus youth conference was in Abilene, Texas. The stake president met us at the airport, dressed in jeans and a western shirt and wearing a bolo tie and boots. He stuck his hand out and with an infectious grin said, "Hah, Ah'm Benny, and this is mah wife, Ginger!" He had his arm affectionately around his beaming wife, and we knew this conference was going to be fun. This wonderful stake leader had organized a youth conference for his fifty youth. Once a year he brought them together, and they came one from a town, one from a high school, in a stake having a four-hundred-mile circumference. There was a rare unity among those young people, and all of us felt it.

As the conference wore on, one young man particularly caught my attention. He was fifteen, blond and refreshingly hand-some. Whenever someone seemed to be shyly standing apart, Jayson would go over to him or her and say, "Why don't you come sit at my table?" "Would you like to go to class with me?" "Why don't you come be on our team?" I wondered if this young man was on the payroll.

The first night at the dance was no different. The youth were mixing happily, but there were still a few shyer ones on the out-skirts of the cultural hall, and I was making the rounds, trying to get them involved. One young lady was standing alone, and per-haps she did not feel as pretty as she would have liked to feel. Perhaps she was not as slim as she wished; perhaps her hair was not as stylish as some of the other girls'. I was talking to her when I felt an arm slip around my shoulders and I looked into the clear blue eyes of this fifteen-year-old Jayson. "Kayathee," he began, with a delicious Texas drawl, "you're just gonna have to do without this young lady for a while because I want to dance with her." And he led her onto the dance floor. He could have danced with her and brought her back to me and felt he had done his part, but Jayson understood more than that. After he had danced with her he got his brother Jeremy to do so, and while Jeremy was dancing he got his other friends to ask her. Without her knowing he had done it, he kept her out there dancing the entire evening. I watched it all and thought, *This young man knows which team he is on.*

The last moments of our youth conferences are spent in a testimony meeting, and in this one Jayson ran up to the front and grabbed the sides of the pulpit. He and his family had moved to California a year earlier, and the boys had now flown back to Abilene to have youth conference with their friends. "California is a big place," he said. "I didn't know what to do with myself." He told us he had felt a little lost until Christmastime, when the ward had organized the youth to gather food donations for a Cambodian branch in his Walnut Creek Stake. They took the sacks of food out to the branch, and Jayson said that felt good, but he looked around at all the little children and wondered what kind of Christmas they were going to have.

He and a friend of his took the ward list and divided it between them. They called the members and asked if they would donate toys that their children didn't use anymore, rummage-sale-type toys, and bring them to the ward party that Friday. Jayson went to the party hoping people had remembered, and peeked up on the stage to see if there was anything there. The stage was mounded with toys, and most of them weren't used at all. The families had made this their family Christmas project, and there were beautiful new toys waiting to be wrapped.

Jayson and his friends literally stayed up all night wrapping the presents, and someone found a big Santa sack to stuff them in and a funny Santa suit to stuff him in. He was a long tall drink of water, so they found pillows to make him look chubby and fat.

The morning after Christmas the youth piled into a car and drove out to the Cambodian branch. Those children came running like chickens for the morning corn. Jayson passed out the toys and chuckled his "ho ho's," and the air was filled with excitement and laughter. Soon it was over and everyone felt warm inside.

Jayson felt a little tug on his Santa suit. He looked down into deep brown eyes and heard a little voice ask, "Does Santa Claus have anything in his sack for me?" Jayson knew it was empty. He did not know why this little boy had missed the earlier festivities, but he swept him up in his arm and whispered in his ear, "Yeah, Santa had me save something special for you!" This incredible young man reached down and took off the watch his father had given him for Christmas the day before. He put it into this little Cambodian boy's hand.

Jayson looked out at us, his Abilene friends, and with tears glistening on his cheeks, he said, "I love the gospel of Jesus Christ." This young man knew what team he was on. In every decision every day he showed it.

$\mathcal{O}$nly What You Give Away

WAYNE B. LYNN

We were surrounded by excitement when my uncle returned from his Tongan mission. Three years is a long time to be gone, and in my tender years my memory of him was dim. I knew him mostly from the colorfully stamped and wrinkled letters that came regularly. There were occasional photographs of him in his white shirt and white pants, with palm trees in the background that fired my imagination. After being carefully passed around for all to see, the pictures were placed in a position of prominence upon the mantel. Sometimes Grandmother received a battered package smelling of mothballs or carrying the musty, damp smell of the islands.

My uncle's homecoming was a great family affair. We were all very proud of him.

A huge, weathered trunk laden with the mysteries of the islands was carried into our large living room. The lid sprang open when unfastened, revealing a bright array of colorful *lava lavas,* seashells, grass skirts, *tapa* cloths, wooden carvings, beaded necklaces, *kava* bowls, and all sorts of romantic memorabilia.

Soon chairs were pushed back and throw rugs moved to the corners of the living room. A huge, elaborately ornamented brown and white tapa cloth was spread out in the center of the floor. We were then seated in a large circle with our bare feet tucked under our folded legs. An exciting chant was given in the Tongan tongue, and we soon joined in. My uncle expertly pounded *kava* in the huge wooden bowl, straining it in a practiced way. After an elaborate ceremony, the half-shell coconut *kava* bowl was finally passed, first to my grandfather and grandmother and then to my mother and father. Eventually, it even came to us lowly children to taste of its bitter, numbing contents.

With this and other ceremonies completed, my uncle began in earnest to unpack his gift-laden trunk. He was lavish in his generosity. My sisters each received grass hula skirts strung with real seashell bands, and necklaces to match. My heart pounded when he handed me a beautiful, sleek, hand-carved canoe. Its tapered sides were ornately carved and etched in white, the outriggers securely fastened with coconut fibers. Small wooden oars made it complete. There were many other handsome gifts, with apparently no one forgotten.

In the years that followed, the precious trunk, which still contained many treasures, was stored in the back room of my grandmother's house while my uncle was living away from home.

One evening, as the school bus dropped us children off near our home, we were astonished to discover our grandparents' house was gone. Nothing was left of the proud, old wooden frame house but smoldering ashes and wisps of smoke. An electrical short in the attic while no one was home had resulted in the destructive fire and total loss of property. Many irreplaceable family photographs, records, and treasures were permanently gone. With a shock we remembered my uncle's chest from the islands. It was only ashes. He had taken none of these things with him.

Several weeks later, most of us almost spontaneously came up with an idea: we would return to him many of the gifts he had given. My boat was a treasured possession on my dressing table, but what fun it was now to be able to give my beloved uncle a gift in return.

Soon his home with his new wife was filled with treasured memories of his mission. He had many beautiful objects, but all he had was what he had given away. The few things he had kept for himself were gone forever.

Our lives are much like this. Really, the only things we take with us are those things we give away.

Friendship
and
Dating

One of the Best Friends
I Ever Had

SHANE BARKER

Donny George was one of the best friends I ever had.

Fifteen years old, he had eyes the color of Windex, and braces that he flashed around as if they were his most prized possession. I first met him while working at Boy Scout camp, and we ended up working together for a couple of years. He was one of the reasons I kept going back year after year.

One time I was busy cutting down weeds at the rifle range when Donny came running up the hill. "Hal sent me to find you," he said, puffing for breath. "They need you down at the lodge for something."

I groaned. I still had another hour or so of work to do on the weeds, and I didn't have time to leave. But I knew that Hal wouldn't send for me if he didn't have to, so I put down my tools and took off.

When I returned an hour later, the weeds had all been cut.

Donny just shrugged when I asked him about it. "They needed to be cut," he said. "So I cut 'em."

That's the kind of friend he was. He made every day fun for me. He made me feel important. He made me feel needed. He made me feel as if I were someone special.

Most important, he brought out the best in me.

"Who Will Be My Friend?"

STEPHEN JASON HALL

The mighty whirl of the helicopter began to die down, and the doors flew open. The paramedics from Life Flight handed me off to the nurses and doctors of the ER at St. Mary's Hospital in Grand Junction, Colorado. With my dad at my side, I was taken into the trauma unit, where I was most certainly the center of attention. The team was doing a barrage of tests, checking my heart, my lungs, my eyes, ears, and nose. X rays were done as well as a blood analysis. As time wore on and the doctors confirmed that my physical condition was stable, the atmosphere lightened a bit and I became the subject of a new set of tests designed to discern how much sensitivity and movement I had lost as a result of a diving accident a few short hours before at Lake Powell, Utah.

The doctor approached me with a small metal instrument that was sharp on one end and dull on the other. He explained to me that he was going to poke me with different sides of this instrument and I was to indicate if I felt the sharp or dull end or anything at all.

I watched the doctor proceed up my foot to my ankle—nothing. I saw him slowly move from my ankle to my knee—still nothing. I wanted to feel something so badly it hurt. I was concentrating with all my might, hoping to feel the prick of his instrument. He continued from my knee to my hip and then from my hip through my midsection to my chest—nothing. It wasn't until he reached under my arm that I felt something. "I felt that! I felt that!" I yelled, so pleased that I had finally felt something. He completed the same test on the other side of my body with the same result, compiled his information, and then left.

A short time later, the doctor returned. With a somberness in his voice that I shall never forget, he explained that his diagnosis was confirmed: I had broken my neck and would never walk again. Although he was 99 percent sure, he said that there was one test left to further support this diagnosis. Soon I was off for a CT scan.

The CT scanner looks like a large white tube. They slide you into the middle of the tube and take in-depth pictures of your body. As I lay in the middle of the tube, the technician explained that he would be in an adjacent room administering the scan and that I must remain completely still.

As I was lying there as still as I possibly could, the room got very quiet and very lonely. In fact, I realized that since my accident earlier that day this was the first time I had been alone. And being alone caused my mind to wander.

I began to wonder what it would be like to live my life in a wheelchair and what changes that would bring—and then real concern set in. I wondered, *Who will want to go to the games with a guy in a wheelchair? Who will date or go to the prom with a guy in a wheelchair? Who will want to just hang out on a Saturday night with a guy in a wheelchair? Who will be my friend?* The answer I received to this last question during the year following my accident has taught me much about friendship and what it truly means to be a friend. I learned that everyone has acquaintances, but only the blessed have friends. I learned that acquaintances and colleagues are a dime a dozen, but true friends are golden. I also learned that these true friends almost always have the same characteristics. If we are willing to use these characteristics as a benchmark, we will more easily be able to discern who our true friends are.

After three months of inpatient stay at the hospital, which were filled with braces, surgery, respirators, and therapy, I was finally released and allowed to go home. The ensuing months taught me a lot about the importance perspective has in friendship.

Before my accident, I was very involved both at school and in my ward—much like most fifteen-year-olds. Athletics was a big part of that involvement. Many of my friends were fellow teammates. We would spend hour upon hour in the weight room, on the practice field, and around the track. Our entire relationship was centered around the games we were preparing to play. When we were together we talked about sports and we watched professionals play the games we dreamed we would one day be a part of, and when our time together was finished we would talk of the games and races that would fill our tomorrows.

Suddenly, after my accident, I found that we no longer had much to talk about. I could no longer join them in practice or battle with them in the crosstown rivalries. And, on top of that, most of these friends were not Latter-day Saints. For most of them, life ended with this life. They had very little concept of a heaven, much less of a resurrection. Those who did have some concept of a God or heaven could not understand how he could allow this tragedy to happen. Our relationships, although strong and important to me, were built on one plane: our athletics. When that plane was gone, there was no perspective to lend any strength to our friendship.

At the same time, I had many Latter-day Saint friends. Although we did not have athletics in common, much of what we did was physical. Dances, ward activities, and all the other daily physical activities teenagers fill their time with were a big part of our friendship. However, when the physical aspects of our relationship were gone, there was something eternal to give our friendship meaning. The fact that we know that there is a God, that his purpose is always for the best, and that there is a resurrection and a place where all ailments will be healed gave our friendship a breadth and depth that could endure the loss of one aspect of our friendship. This eternal perspective was essential to the continuity of our care and concern for each other.

This is not to say that our only friends should be Latter-day Saints. But we must realize that only relationships with perspective and an understanding of what is truly important will last. We must seek after relationships that will foster this perspective, and we must strive to be the kind of friend that endures forever.

I first met Kolette in my junior year at Brigham Young University. We became fast friends. As we began to date, our relationship started to become more and more special to both of us. We began to spend all our free time together. Whenever either of us had a few extra minutes, we searched for ways to spend those minutes in the company of the other. As our relationship grew, it became evident that a decision of marriage was most definitely in the future. People who were very close to Kolette began to ask her if she could really handle being married to someone in a wheelchair. Out of concern for her, they filled her mind with questions she had not yet dealt with. Suddenly, every time we were together she began to wonder if she could live her life with a man in a wheelchair, if she could be happy in a relationship in which the responsibility for everything from mowing the lawn to teaching the kids to play football would fall on her shoulders.

All of this questioning caused Kolette a lot of concern. But, as she took some time for private contemplation and sincere prayer, she found her answer. She learned that she was asking the wrong kinds of questions. The question that really mattered was, "Do I love Jason?" If she could answer that question affirmatively, then the answers to the other questions would come easily. She had to decide if she cared about what was essential about me: my spirit and my heart. Everything physical was secondary. She could deal with the fact that I couldn't stand if she knew she loved me.

Six months later we were married. We are happier now than we can ever remember. How grateful I am for my sweetheart, who chose to have an eternal perspective.

Sometimes when we choose the people who will fill our lives as friends, we are tempted to first answer the questions that Kolette was confronted with—but all those things are physical. We worry about who is the most popular, who has the most money, or who is the most beautiful. Because the eternal does not come naturally, we often look first to the captain of the football team or the head cheerleader as we try to find friends.

Although there are plenty of football stars and homecoming queens who are wonderful people, when we seek friends we must first look at the hearts and souls of those we choose to be a part of our inner circle.

If we find people who are striving to live a righteous life, show a genuine concern and love for others, and have an eternal perspective, whether they are at the top or bottom of the social ladder, they will be friends to last a lifetime, come what may.

Hanging Out with the Ugly Jumpers

LISA H. OLSEN

The sun setting behind the mountains cast a golden glow on the outdoor arena. Spotlights highlighted the competition floor as the audience sat silently. Male competitors waited nervously backstage, sizing up the competition. It was the perfect night for the international contest! Weeks of eliminations had narrowed the field to three athletes. I waited quietly and whispered to my friends, trying to decide which routine Richard would use for freestyle competition.

The announcer broke the tension: "Welcome, ladies and gentlemen. Our first competitor is Richard Glazier, representing the United States."

Just then Richard appeared at the top of a beautifully groomed hill and waved to his cheering fans. With confidence he descended to the competition floor. His face was serious; he wanted this title. Saluting the judges to acknowledge the beginning of his routine, he placed his hands on the edge of the apparatus. All eyes followed closely as he pulled himself onto the trampoline and began to flop and turn like a suffocating fish.

With one last, great spasm, Richard landed perfectly upright and began to bounce, his arms held in perfectly choreographed unison. Richard then fell on his back, bounced back up, and attempted a toe-touch. After a few somersaults he jumped up, still swaying from the motion of the trampoline, and saluted the judges, who held up their score cards: perfect tens! The audience—all eight of us—broke out cheering, knowing that Richard had clearly done a jump so ugly that neither Trent nor John could possibly equal it. It was summer again, time for the ugly jump contests in Mark's backyard.

As I remember such experiences with my friends, I am convinced that I had a highly unique (albeit a little strange) group of outstanding friends. I was especially lucky to count among them many young men who were "just friends." I am now thirty, and I work with teenagers daily. I watch many young women struggle with identity and work to figure out how to fit in.

As a teenager I felt I had a lot going for me: I had a wonderful family, I maintained good grades, I had good friends, and I was very involved in school extracurricular activities. But I still felt like a social misfit. I had plenty of girlfriends, and, just like many of them, my thoughts frequently turned to boys. Also, I worried too much about appearance because I didn't look like all the popular girls. I had naturally curly hair that was impossible to control, I wore braces from seventh grade until I was a junior in high school, I wore glasses (I should say I was *supposed* to wear glasses, because I never put them on at school), I didn't have much fashion sense (but neither did anyone else in the early eighties), and I didn't live in the chic part of town. Because of my exploding curly hair, boys would joke and call me "peach fuzz." When I cut my hair very short, it made me look about forty, so the boys started to call me "Miss Mature" and thought they were pretty funny.

When I turned sixteen, I thought boys would be able to see beyond my appearance and ask me out, but this was not the case. Instead, I was a very disappointed girl on my seventeenth birthday when I was still waiting for my first date. I had spent far too much desire and worry on wanting to date, and I knew that something had to change: me. I had to adjust my attitude and outlook. If boys weren't going to ask me out, then I was going to make them my friends. This proved to be one of the best resolves I ever made.

I also learned that Church leaders and General Authorities wanted me to make friends with young men and relax on the romance. For example, President Spencer W. Kimball specifically advised: "Dating and especially steady dating in the early teens is most hazardous. It distorts the whole picture of life. It deprives the youth of worthwhile and rich experiences; it limits friendships; it reduces the acquaintance which can be so valuable in selecting a partner for time and eternity" (*The Teachings of Spencer W. Kimball,* ed. Edward L. Kimball [Salt Lake City: Bookcraft, 1982], p. 289). Steady dating limits friendships! Had I been a frequent dater in high school, I would have missed out on wonderful *friendships* with Steve, McKay, Jon, Scott, Dave, Paul, and of course the ugly jumpers.

Steve was the junior class president. He worked to make me an honorary member of student government; I had run for office every year but was never elected, so it was a thrill to still be involved somehow. Because I was an artist, he put me on every dance committee to work on decorations. During planning stages and the late decorating nights, I formed great friendships with many people. Steve was constantly inviting me and my friends Sara and Joanne to all his parties. McKay and Jon were friends I made through A Cappella who became like big brothers to me. Dave and Paul were best buddies I met while on the seminary council. And then there was Scott. I don't even remember the classes we had together or the things we talked about; I just remember that he was my knight in shining armor on the day of the junior prom. As with other dances, I had worked for hours on the decorations for this prom but was dateless. Scott had not planned on going to the prom because he was a senior, but, knowing how hard I had worked and how much I wanted to go to the prom, he came to my door one hour after the prom had started and whisked me to the dance. We had a great time—as friends.

I was also lucky to have three wonderful girlfriends: Ruth, Joanne, and Sara, who were all from my ward. Somehow we later merged with the ugly jumpers, John, Rich, and Mark. Sara described our friendships this way: "I looked at my guys as my friends, not as potential romances. They were like brothers but closer to our own age. They were the good boys next door. It was more fun to go with them as friends than to have a tantalizing romance, even if such a thing were possible."

Besides, romances make you worried, and you try to impress. We didn't entertain physical attractions, so we didn't feel inhibited. This attitude was more conducive to friendship.

One evening, while I was serving at a girlfriend's wedding reception, Mark, Rich, and John came into the kitchen to keep me company. As I wrote in my journal: "They came and sat in the kitchen with us for over an hour. Rich and John had a cream puff stuffing contest: Rich ate a whole cream puff in one bite, then John put two in his mouth, and then Rich stuffed in three in one bite. It was disgusting! After the reception we went up to Haley's house to order pizza and watch *North Avenue Irregulars*. As we were leaving, our attention turned to a sheet cake. Rich grabbed a piece with his bare hands and put the whole thing in his mouth. John, not wanting to be outdone, shoved in two whole pieces. Then Rich stuffed in three and kissed Haley, smearing frosting all over her face. As if things couldn't get worse, John actually put four pieces in his mouth. Typical." Obviously, these boys weren't out to impress us.

Our group spent endless hours together. As we all look back, we remember that most of our time was spent talking. It was fun to listen to the guys open up and actually share their thoughts and feelings (I never experienced that on a first, or second, or third date). These talks were especially memorable when we would go up on Mark's roof for what we called a "roof sit," a long night of only talking, or when we would ride the mopeds to the temple grounds to talk. Other great memories include: making movies and editing them at Mark's father's studio; the girls kidnapping John, tying him up, blindfolding him, putting him on the doorstep of a girl he liked, ringing the bell, and leaving John behind (it later went down in history as our group's best practical joke); passing out copies of the Book of Mormon in Las Vegas; enjoying formal Christmas dinners at Ruth Ann's house; and trying to take over the world in a game of Risk (our group's official game). These young men were the best friends I could have ever asked for. I treasure their friendships—they even helped me form an idea about the kind of man I would eventually like to marry.

From ugly jump contests to the last-minute junior prom, I have fond memories of my male *friends* and will be forever grateful for their friendships and love.

$\mathscr{T}$hat's What Friends Are For

VICKEY PAHNKE

$\mathbf{W}$ho are your friends? And how do you know? Do they bring out the best in you? Are they there for you when you need them? Have you ever been burned by someone you thought you could trust? What are friends for, anyway?

Life can be a lot easier when we have friends to share with us, cry with us, laugh with us, and reassure us that we are okay . . . even when we make mistakes.

My daughter once said to me: "Mom, I'm so embarrassed I could just die. I'll never be able to hang around with my friends again." I told her: "Honey, embarrassing moments run in our family. Your friends know to expect such things from you. And, Andrea, if a person could die from embarrassment, I would have been dead a long time ago."

You need to understand that my life has been a series of humiliating incidents. When I first came to Utah as a student I decided I would leave the "old" me at home in Virginia and start anew. This was flawed thinking—I failed to realize that I was bringing myself with me. Let me illustrate.

At my first ward meeting at BYU I saw this awesome guy, a really good-looking returned missionary. He seemed to have credibility because he was the ward clerk. What could I do to catch his eye? Was I in luck! As a member of the Relief Society presidency, I had been asked to speak in church the next Sunday. Here was my chance to prepare diligently, deliver sweetly, and impress this young man with my spirituality! (Yes, I know my reasoning left something to be desired.) On Sunday, as I stood at the podium, I looked down on the front row to see "my" young man grinning up at me. As I shared my remarks we exchanged smiles. I thought, *Yes! This is working! He wants to know who I am!*

I concluded, and as I began confidently down the steps that would take me directly past him, the heel broke on my shoe. I slid down the steps, sprawling at the feet of the young ward clerk. Agghh! The truth was out! Now the entire ward knew the real me—I was as klutzy in Utah as I had been in Virginia. I was *so* embarrassed. It didn't take long for everyone to learn that if they wanted to have fun they should hang around me . . . *something* would happen that would make them laugh.

Just the next week we decided to go roller-skating. What a blast! I had never done this before! At that time I had very long hair, which can be a pain to wash and style every day. For the outing I decided to put a zillion pins in my hair to hold it up, and wear a wig.

As the others skated with great abandon I clung to the railing for dear life. But gradually, with confidence growing, I let go and picked up a little speed. This was fun! This was awesome! I could do it! I didn't realize that at one spot in the rink the flooring didn't quite fit together. As I skated along, increasing in pace and confidence, I hit this uneven flooring. My feet flew up, I landed on my backside, and the wig flew off my head.

The whole place came to a standstill. Everyone simultaneously stifled a laugh-gasp. The fellow who skates around to keep order came to me, picked up my wig, and asked, "Does this belong to you?" I was so embarrassed I thought I would die. But I didn't . . . I merely provided another good laugh for my new friends.

Through many episodes like these I learned an important lesson about my friends: they accepted me for who I was. What a blessing it was to feel loved and cared about even with my obvious imperfections! Because of their acceptance, my friends helped me to accept myself. I learned that friends make it easier to get back up after we've fallen down, and start over again. Isn't that what friends are for? To love us and help us learn to better love ourselves? Good friends make all the difference.

The Obligation of Friendship

EDGAR A. GUEST

You ought to be fine for the sake of the folks
  Who think you are fine.
If others have faith in you doubly you're bound
  To stick to the line.
It's not only on you that dishonor descends:
You can't hurt yourself without hurting your friends.

You ought to be true for the sake of the folks
  Who believe you are true.
You never should stoop to a deed that your friends
  Think you wouldn't do.
If you're false to yourself, be the blemish but small,
You have injured your friends; you've been false to them all.

For friendship, my boy, is a bond between men
  That is founded on truth:
It believes in the best of the ones that it loves,
  Whether old man or youth;
And the stern rule it lays down for me and for you
Is to be what our friends think we are, through and through.

Am I in Love?

CARLOS E. ASAY

In answer to the question, "How may I know when I am in love?" President David O. McKay quoted a friend as saying: "My mother once said that if you meet a girl in whose presence you feel a desire to achieve, who inspires you to do your best, and to make the most of yourself, such a young woman is worthy of your love and is awakening love in your heart." President McKay added: "I submit that as a true guide. In the presence of the girl you truly love you do not feel to grovel; in her presence you do not attempt to take advantage of her; in her presence you feel that you would like to be everything that a 'Master Man' should become, for she will inspire you to that ideal" (*Gospel Ideals* [Salt Lake City: Improvement Era, 1953], p. 459).

I used this "true guide" of President McKay's on one occasion when I was counselling a young lady. This particular coed, a beauty queen, rose to the head of my class at the beginning of a semester and toward the middle came dangerously close to failing. I met with her and asked why her performance in class had dropped so suddenly. She guessed that her problem was related to her courtship—a courtship that seemed directed toward marriage.

I had an uneasy feeling about my student's situation, so I asked: "Do you really love the young man you are dating, and does he really love you?" After a short pause, she replied, "I think so." I wondered if she had heard of President McKay's "goodness test" of love. She had not. I therefore applied it by asking some questions.

"What has happened to your studies since you began dating seriously?"

"I'm failing all of my classes," she admitted.

I said, "Is that good?"

"No," she confessed, "that isn't so good."

"What has happened to your church attendance and activity in recent weeks?"

"My boyfriend isn't all that religious. We often skip church on Sunday."

"Is that good?"

"No, that isn't good."

"Final question," I added. "What has happened to your relationships with roommates and family members of late?"

She lowered her head and said: "My boyfriend is very jealous of my time and tries to monopolize my life. As a result of this, I am not as close to my friends and family as I should be."

"Is that good?"

"No," she said once more, "that is not good."

"My dear," I concluded, "I do not need to ask any more questions. Your intended has failed miserably the goodness test of love. Do be careful. Don't make a mistake that may blight your life eternally."

It was obvious to me that the young man's professed love was mocked by his actions. His influence upon the girl was not positive or building; nor did it suggest that he was making any sacrifice in her behalf. What he was doing to her was actually cruel, selfish, and abusive. His was a pseudo-love.

The young lady left my office with tears in her eyes, making me wonder if my advice had been too blunt. A few days later, however, she came bounding into my classroom with renewed spirit and a smile on her face and announced, "I gave him the boot and I haven't felt this good in a long time."

Packin' Friends

STEPHEN JASON HALL

I will not soon forget my first real backpacking adventure as a young Boy Scout (before the diving accident that left me paralyzed from the chest down). I had procrastinated preparing for the event until just an hour before we were to leave, so I didn't worry about what would be lightest or most simple to pack—I just packed. First I grabbed the tightly rolled sleeping bag and foam pad from the storage closet. Although I had never practiced rolling them myself, I figured it couldn't be too hard and that I could learn after we reached the campsite. After throwing some clothes in, I had to worry about food. Since I had no desire to eat anything dehydrated, I quickly ran to the pantry and grabbed four cans of Spaghettios and a six-pack of Sprite. I knew these items would be heavy, but I had to pack them only one way, and I was sure we'd have a garbage can nearby where I could throw away the empty cans. Finally, all packed and ready to go, I grabbed my brand-new hiking boots out of their box and ran out the door.

The five miles into camp weren't too bad. My backpack weighed a lot, but I was rested and made the trip without incident. Although my new boots made my feet tender in a few places, we had a wonderful time on the camp out—but by the end of the weekend, those tender areas were blisters. And although the Spaghettios tasted good, there was no trash can to be found and I had to find a way to pack the empty cans out of the camp. Unfortunately, trash always seems to take up more room, so there was no longer any room on my backpack for the foam pad and it therefore ended up under my arm. The sleeping bag I packed out resembled the one I packed in only because they were the same color; it was so loosely rolled that it barely fit on top of my pack.

As we left that site, I was completely unprepared for the five miles that lay ahead. And it went from bad to worse. The blisters on my feet became so painful that I had to finish the trek with only one boot on. Not long after that, my loosely rolled sleeping bag unrolled so that one end was dragging through the mud; it looked more like a wedding veil than a sleeping bag. Needless to say, I was a sight—and I was beginning to lag way behind. It got bad enough that I was willing to endure any humiliation that asking for help might create. Each of the boys ahead, all of whom purported to be my friends, were too busy or preoccupied to help me—all except one.

Unlike me, Mark was prepared. His backpack looked great. Realizing that my packing job was probably unsalvageable at this stage of the game, he carried my foam pad and my garbage so that my sleeping bag would fit inside my backpack with my clothes. Mark's journey back to the vehicles was substantially more difficult than it needed to be. He was prepared, and I was not. But he was willing to endure a little pain to help me— because he was my friend.

It is easy to find friends who will be with us when the sun shines. What we must work diligently to do is find, and be, the kind of friends who are willing to make the sacrifices necessary to stick together when life gets stormy.

Being a Friend First

ARDETH G. KAPP

Years ago when I had just turned sixteen, I left my small hometown of Glenwood, Alberta, Canada, which has a population of approximately three hundred people. I went away for my senior year of high school because the courses I needed for graduation were not available to me at home. I knew only one person in my new school, and I was scared. I hadn't had any experience in making friends except with those kids I had grown up with. I didn't wear the latest fashions like the other girls, so I looked different. I wasn't a part of the in-group or of any group, for that matter. I was away from home, homesick, and lonesome. Even if they had asked me, I didn't have the money to do the things the other kids did. I yearned for friends. There was so much talking going on, it seemed that everyone else had lots of friends. *How do you get in?* I wondered. No one was discourteous, but I felt ignored, as if they didn't know I was there.

Can you imagine how desperately I wanted friends, or at least one friend? I remember feeling alone, a long way from home. Kneeling by my bed day after day, night and morning, I prayed for friends, I pleaded for friends. I wanted boyfriends, girlfriends, young and older friends, member and nonmember friends. I felt I needed friends for my survival. I talked to my Father in Heaven and promised that in every way I would strive to do what was right no matter what, if I could just be helped to know how to make friends in my new situation. The thought came to my mind that maybe there were others who felt as I did; maybe I should try to forget about myself and be a friend first. I thought, *I can smile, and I can say hi.*

I believe that thought was a whispering of the Spirit in answer to my prayer. I began to focus on being a friend instead of having a friend. I listened to the Spirit. I did smile, and I said hi to everyone. I learned to be friendly. At first it was hard, but before long it became easier. At the end of my senior year, I was nominated by the student body as the representative girl for the high school where I had attended only one year. Some may have considered it a popularity victory, but I'll always know it was in answer to the fervent prayer of a sixteen-year-old who learned how to be friends with everybody.

The Making of Friends

EDGAR A. GUEST

If nobody smiled and nobody cheered and nobody helped us
along,
If each every minute looked after himself and good things all
went to the strong,
If nobody cared just a little for you, and nobody thought about
me,
And we stood all alone to the battle of life, what a dreary old
world it would be!

If there were no such a thing as a flag in the sky as a symbol of
comradeship here,
If we lived as the animals live in the woods, with nothing held
sacred or dear,
And selfishness ruled us from birth to the end, and never a neighbor had we,
And never we gave to another in need, what a dreary old world
it would be!

Oh, if we were rich as the richest on earth and strong as the
strongest that lives,
Yet never we knew the delight and the charm of the smile which
the other man gives,
If kindness were never a part of ourselves, though we owned all
the land we could see,
And friendship meant nothing at all to us here, what a dreary old
world it would be!

Life is sweet just because of the friends we have made and the
things which in common we share;
We want to live on not because of ourselves, but because of the
people who care;
It's giving and doing for somebody else—on that all life's splen-
dor depends,
And the joy of this world, when you've summed it all up, is found
in the making of friends.

Faith
and
Prayer

"You Can't Pray a Lie"

BRAD WILCOX

During my junior year in high school we were reading *The Adventures of Huckleberry Finn,* by Mark Twain. It was Thursday night. I knew there was a test Friday, so I brushed my teeth, kissed Mom and Dad good night, grabbed my book, and took off to my bedroom. I was almost twenty-five pages behind in assigned reading. I had to catch up, and catch up that night! I knelt down hurriedly by the side of my bed and whipped off some absurd, insincere thing that I was willing to let pass as a prayer. Then, climbing into bed and opening my book, I began reading the words the author put into the mouth of Huck Finn:

"I about made up my mind to pray, and see if I couldn't try to quit being the kind of boy I was and be better. So I kneeled down. But the words wouldn't come. Why wouldn't they? It warn't no use to try and hide it from Him. . . . I knowed very well why they wouldn't come. It was because my heart warn't right; it was because . . . I was holding on to the biggest [sin] of all. I was tryin' to make my mouth *say* I would do the right thing and the clean thing . . . but deep down in me I knowed it was a lie, and He knowed it. You can't pray a lie—I found that out."

Needless to say, I dropped back down on my knees and asked forgiveness for my insincerity. Now, when it is late and I am tired, when I kneel down offering a prayer with just words and no real feeling, I climb between the sheets and remember Huck Finn and the lesson we both had to recognize, that an insincere prayer is worthless. "You can't pray a lie."

$\mathcal{P}$raying for Jack

MARK A. BYBEE

$\mathbf{A}$s nearly as I can recall, the first miracle I ever personally witnessed took place when I was about eleven years old. It happened in front of our home in Columbus, Ohio. As the car stopped across the street from our home, Jack, my younger brother, jumped out of the back door on the curb side, and I heard my mom yell, "Jack, wait on the curb." But Jack ignored Mom, and as I looked over my right shoulder from the backseat I saw him dart between the rear of the car we were in and the parked car behind us. I remember getting my head turned around just in time to see a big car run smack over the top of Jack. His head smashed out the headlight, and then the car ran right over him.

I'll never forget the feeling of incredible fright which ran through me as I saw his little body flying through the air. I wanted to scream and turn back the clock as I saw the five-year-old body come to a rest in a clump on the side of the road. I screamed out, "No!" as I flung the door open and ran to his side. Everything inside of me told me not to touch him, because if I moved him I might cause paralysis. Jack didn't move, and he was bleeding from his head. I turned back toward the car just in time to get between Jack and my mom as she ran screaming, "My baby, my baby." I held her by her arms and pushed against her as I tried to get her not to touch Jack. She finally calmed down and told me to run and get Dad.

Dad was at the kitchen counter, having paid no attention to the screeching tire sounds since they were so common. I yelled to him that Jack had been hit, and he flew out the front door and went straight to his side to check his vital signs. As Dad knelt down he asked me to take Mom inside and pray for Jack.

I'll remember forever the scene of my brothers and sisters kneeling around the sofa praying out loud for Jack. I couldn't stay there, so I ran back out and stood by my dad. I watched as Dad felt for a pulse and listened at Jack's chest. When he looked up at me with a look of futility and deep sadness as he said, "Go comfort your mother," I knew Jack was dead and I didn't want it to be so. As I walked slowly from Jack and Dad, I looked back to see Dad praying with his head down. As nearly as I can recall, Dad was praying that Jack could live and that he could raise his son to manhood. Then by his priesthood authority he commanded Jack to live. I looked down again at Jack, and his little body just lay motionless on the ground.

I went back inside and knelt next to my mom. I didn't have the heart to say anything. The next thing I remember is hearing the sounds of the sirens in the distance. We all jumped up and ran outside as the ambulance pulled up next to Jack and the drivers jumped out and ran to Jack's side.

I well recall the scene of Jack sitting up coughing and crying as he held his head and complained of a headache. The attendants put Jack into the ambulance and then sped off to the hospital. Dad said that Jack was seriously injured, with possible broken bones and other injuries.

You can imagine our surprise when Jack returned with a concussion and no broken bones.

$\mathcal{P}$at

JACK R. CHRISTIANSON

Ifirst met Pat while playing football at Weber State University. I was sitting in the locker room, preparing for spring practice, when he walked in with some other recruits and one of our coaches. He was a defensive back being recruited from a junior college in southern California.

I'll never forget my first impression of him. I almost got sick! He walked in, strutting as if he had just descended from the heavens. He wore a large-brimmed Hawaiian straw hat with a piece of flowered cloth wrapped around the top that was similar to his flowered Hawaiian shirt. The shirt was unbuttoned in the front, showing a gold chain swishing in the dark hairs of his chest. He wore close-fitting white shorts. His feet sported thongs, and his upper lip, a well-trimmed mustache. He was handsome. If you don't believe me, you could ask him.

Before leaving California he had been warned about Mormons. He had been told that they all wore black hats, long dark coats, and the sort of buckle shoes the Pilgrims wore, and that all the men had more than one wife. When he found out that I was a Mormon, the fireworks started. He verbally tortured me, most of his remarks being cynical, cutting, or degrading. There were times when he sounded sincere, but they were rare. I was usually a sucker, however, for his seemingly sincere questions. I hoped each time that maybe *this* time he would be genuinely curious. When the smart-alecky comments would come, I tried not to show my pain or anger. I would laugh along with him, punch him softly in the shoulder, and tell him he was crazy.

It was a difficult relationship. The fact that he was a defensive back and I was a quarterback didn't help. We were forced into physical conflict during practice. The tension mounted daily. To make things worse, we rode together on the bus and often roomed together on road trips.

After practice one night the two of us were alone in the shower room. I didn't want to talk, but he kept asking me questions. Finally he asked me how many wives I really had. As he asked, my mind raced. I knew I shouldn't lead him on, but I thought he deserved some of his own medicine. He had been so cruel that I thought I would get him back a little.

As I turned the water off and reached for a towel, I looked in all directions as if to make sure we were alone. I could see from the excitement in his eyes that he really thought he was on to something no one else knew.

"You promise you won't tell anyone, Pat? I mean, I could get put in jail if anyone found out."

His eyes widened in anticipation. "I swear! I swear! You can trust me."

Sure, I thought. Then I said to him: "I have seven. But you can't say a word!"

"You've gotta be kidding me! I knew it, Christianson! I knew it!"

I asked him if he would like to come to dinner and meet them. Of course he agreed. The next night after practice I drove him to our apartment. My wife had fixed a beautiful dinner. After dinner I told him the truth, that Melanie was my only wife. He was angry and left. He wouldn't even let me give him a ride back to his apartment. Afterwards, his teasing and taunting worsened.

Sometimes I would come home from practice and tell my wife, "If I don't come home tomorrow, it's because I'll be in jail."

"Oh dear, what have you done?"

"Nothing yet, but if Pat says one more word about the Church or the Savior, I'm going to kill him!"

I would go back to practice and Pat's taunting would continue. I continued to smile and act as if it didn't bother me.

Then one night, after a game with Long Beach State University, the team was riding home from the airport in a bus. It was about one or two in the morning. The ride was terribly uncomfortable, especially for those with bruises and injuries. I was sitting next to Pat, as usual. He was sound asleep with his head tilted to the back of the seat, his mouth gaping open. I couldn't sleep, so I was leaning forward with my face in my hands, looking at the floor. As I gazed at the floor, not really thinking of anything, I spotted a white stick under the seat in front of me. For some reason, I reached down and brought it up to where I could see it in the light. On the end was about half of a cherry sucker. Like a magnet, it had attracted much of the hair and dirt from the floor of the bus.

As I looked at it again, my mind raced. I looked at Pat and then at the sucker. His mouth was still wide open and his head bobbed with every jolt of the bus.

I knew that I shouldn't seek revenge and that I should just forget everything from the past, but I didn't. I got some other teammates to watch the dastardly deed. It was much more enjoyable to share the fun! Several of us gathered around Pat. I pulled a long hair off the sucker and then carefully lowered the sucker into his mouth and laid it on his tongue! He made a brief noise and swatted at his face with one hand, but didn't wake up. All of us who were awake tried to muffle our laughter, but it was impossible.

I then took the hair and began to pull it across his nose and lips. In his sleep he kept swatting at the nuisance the way you would swat a fly on a summer afternoon. Finally he woke up and nearly got sick when he removed the sucker from his mouth and realized what it was. He didn't think it was too funny, but we all roared. I told him I would never get mad when he teased me; I would just get even.

Something strange happened after that night. The teasing virtually ceased, and Pat and I became the best of friends. He played ward softball and basketball with me and spent many evenings in our apartment. Of course, he warned us that he was born a Catholic and would die a Catholic, so we shouldn't try to convert him.

Pat didn't play football during our senior year. I don't remember all the details, just that he had hurt his arm in an accident. Our coach also was fired and there were some changes.

As he prepared to leave for home, Melanie and I went to visit him one last time. We had written our testimonies in a copy of the Book of Mormon and wanted to give it to him as a parting gift.

When we told him we wanted to give him a gift, he asked, "Is it a book?"

"Yes."

"Is it the Book of Mormon?"

"Yes."

"Well, you'd better give it to someone else who'll read it, so it won't be wasted."

I talked him into taking it, but he grudgingly wrapped it in a brown paper bag and threw it in his suitcase. We said good-bye and didn't see Pat again for about two years.

By then I had graduated from Weber State and was teaching and coaching in Salt Lake City. About a week before Christmas I received a phone call. It was Pat, wanting to know if I was still a Mormon and if he could come to Utah to talk to me.

I asked him why he called me. He said, "No matter how much I teased you or made fun of you, you never got mad or upset."

Little did he know I wanted to kill him nearly every day we played ball together!

He went on: "You know that book you gave me? Well, I've been reading it, and I have a ton of questions I need to ask you."

I responded that there were many sets of missionaries in the Los Angeles area who would be thrilled to answer all of his questions. He said he didn't want to talk to the missionaries. He wanted to talk to me.

I suggested that he talk to a Mormon bishop in his area. He responded, "I have been! That's the problem. He answers every question I ask him, and I'm mixed up. Jack, I'm not sure anymore that my church is true."

I wanted to tell him I could have told him that years ago, but I held my tongue.

Finally we agreed that he could come to our place in Salt Lake City for Christmas. Two days later, with his car stuffed with everything he owned, he stood on our doorstep. Melanie and I thought he would stay only a few days, but he stayed nearly six months. We had a great time.

Pat was ready to hear the gospel. It happened that two full-time missionaries lived just across the street from us. They taught the gospel to Pat. I was able to participate in the teaching. Pat did his part. He read the Book of Mormon faithfully and prayed with a sincere heart. At the end of the following February he decided to be baptized. The entire ward had grown to love him and was excited for the sacred event to take place.

The day of Pat's baptism arrived. It was Saturday. As we ate breakfast that morning, Pat suddenly asked, "Jack, do you know where President Kimball lives?"

I replied, "Yeah, I've driven by a few times."

"Do you think he's home?"

"Well, I don't know, Pat. He's the prophet of the whole world, you know."

"I think he's home, and I want to invite him to my baptism tonight."

I tried to explain that you just don't go to the prophet's house and invite him to your baptism. But Pat wouldn't accept that answer. He talked me into taking him to President Kimball's home.

It was a cold morning. As we pulled up to the curb, Pat jumped out of the car even before it had stopped. As he approached the door, two security men met him and informed him that President Kimball wasn't feeling well and had asked not to be disturbed. Pat was not so easily dissuaded. He tried again and again. Finally he walked back to the car.

We discussed the situation and decided that a note might accomplish our purpose. I asked the gentlemen if we could leave a note for the prophet. One of them replied, "Sure, but I can't guarantee he'll get it today."

Pat rolled down his window and shouted, "He better get it today!"

I tried to settle him down.

We didn't have any paper in the car, and Pat was too stubborn to ask the security men for some, so we finally used the only thing we had—a Dairy Queen napkin we found in the glove compartment. Pat scribbled a brief note, folded the napkin, then wrote on the outside: "To President Kimball from Pat." He then walked up to the security people, handed them the note, and said, "He'd better get it today!"

When we returned home we had quite a talk about proper Church etiquette. I don't think it mattered very much to him.

The hour for the baptism finally arrived. We were all a little nervous. The thought that Pat had invited the prophet and the thought that he just might come was somewhat unnerving.

Pat delayed the start of the meeting. He was certain President Kimball would come. The bishop insisted we start; another baptism was scheduled after Pat's. Pat was convinced that if President Kimball had received the note he would be there. He asked the bishop if, before we proceeded, he and I could take time to pray. The bishop agreed, but asked us to hurry.

I don't remember the exact words of Pat's prayer as we, all dressed in white, knelt on that cold, wet tile floor, but I will never forget the feeling I had. He prayed something like this: "Father in Heaven, I know this church is true. That's why I'm joining it. I also know President Kimball is your prophet and that you talk with him. Would you please tell him that I'm being baptized tonight, and that if he doesn't hurry he's going to miss it!"

At the end of the prayer we embraced, and I led Pat into the font. He looked for the prophet all the way into the water. No prophet. He looked again when he came up out of the water. No prophet.

Several minutes later we placed our hands on Pat's wet head and confirmed him a member of The Church of Jesus Christ of Latter-day Saints. Again, he looked around. Again, no prophet. We stayed afterwards for dinner and then went home. Pat was quiet. Melanie and I knew he was disappointed that the prophet had not attended.

A couple of months later I came home from work and Melanie was ecstatic. As I drove the car into our parking spot she ran out to meet me. In her hand was a letter. After greeting me she showed me the letter. It was addressed to Pat at our address. The return address was written: "SWK, Office of the First Presidency, 47 E. South Temple." I was shocked! Melanie held the envelope up to the sunlight to see if she could read anything on the inside. She jokingly suggested that we steam it open and read it, then seal it up again. We decided to wait for Pat to read this once-in-a-lifetime letter from God's prophet, seer, and revelator.

When Pat arrived home that evening, the letter lay under his silverware. He picked it up almost playfully; but as he viewed the return address, things clicked in his mind. "SWK, SWK, What the . . .?"

He quickly ripped it open and began to read. I remember approximately what he read: "Dear Pat, I just received your letter on the napkin this morning. Please forgive me for being so busy. If I had received it on the day of your baptism I would have been honored to attend. The Church is now yours as much as it is mine, and I would like to give you several suggestions to help you keep your testimony strong."

He then listed several items, such as prayer, scripture study, family home evening, service, and so on. The letter closed with, "I love you, Pat. I love you. Your eternal friend, Spencer Woolley Kimball."

All three of us sat weeping.

Pat read the letter over and over. A personal letter from the prophet! All of us were stunned.

He later showed the letter to the bishop and asked if he could read it to the ward in Sunday School and bear his testimony. I realize that that isn't general Church procedure, but thank goodness for a bishop with wisdom and understanding. He told Pat he could have five minutes at the end of the meeting.

I will never forget what happened that morning in Salt Lake City. Pat came to the pulpit and said something to this effect: "I received a letter from a friend of mine. Most of you have heard of him. His name is Spencer W. Kimball."

Most of those in the congregation laughed under their breath, knowing that Pat was a joker. I'm sure most of them thought he was kidding. But when he began to read the letter, they became silent. As he finished reading the prophet's closing expression of love, very few were not deeply touched. Then Pat bore a beautiful and powerful testimony, declaring, "I know that President Kimball is a prophet just like Moses or Abraham. Only prophets do things like this. He didn't forget me!"

Approximately a year later I helped ordain Pat to be an elder. A year or so after that I sat in the Salt Lake Temple and witnessed Pat and his beautiful wife being sealed to each other and then to their lovely baby daughter. It was wonderful!

"*I* Was Thirsty . . ."

MARION D. HANKS

Rosalie was new in the ward. At fifteen this can be a problem. Everyone had his own friends. All the groups were settled. Everyone knew for sure just which boys or girls went around together. They all went to the same school. And they'd all lived in the same area for ages, it seemed. They had so much in common. They had so many things to talk about, so much to laugh at. They looked so busy with plans to make and places to go and the weekend's activities to report on. It was like being surrounded by water but not being able to drink.

Being new to Rosalie meant being out of it. She wished her parents had never moved away from the ward where she had become converted to the Church and where she had felt so welcomed. How thirsty she was for friends and fun and a feeling of belonging!

It was just before Christmas, and the holiday held no excitement for her. She had promised herself last night as she finished her prayers that if things weren't better at church this week, she'd never come back again. She just couldn't take any more sitting alone, having no one to talk with, no one to walk to class with. Oh, the kids had said hello that first time, and the teacher had welcomed her, but that was the end of that.

What Rosalie didn't know was that someone else had also been praying last night. Her mother sensed this trying problem in Rosalie's life and had earnestly asked Heavenly Father to help, to touch someone's heart that they might take this young girl in so she wouldn't be lost to the kingdom.

That Sunday when Rosalie slipped into her place on one side

of the chapel, she wasn't alone for long. One of the most popular girls in the ward left the familiar group she always came in with and walked over toward Rosalie.

"Hi!" She smiled broadly as she sat down beside her. "May I sit here?"

"Oh, yes, do! Isn't Christmas a happy time?" Rosalie uttered a silent prayer of thanks that there was one girl in the many who would bother to offer just the kind of drink that would quench her particular thirst.

$\mathcal{F}$or a Greater Purpose

JOHN CRISTEN CRAWFORD

We were on our way to Mammoth Mountain, California, where we planned to enjoy a wonderful week of ski racing and fun in the snow. Just as we were entering Tonapah, Nevada, the driver of the car asked me to take the wheel for a minute. Three of us were in the car. The third member in the backseat grabbed the wheel in a joking manner, turning it almost completely around. The car spun from side to side on the road, finally going off a ten- or fifteen-foot ledge. I was thrown from the car after it left the road; seconds later the big Travelall rolled over me.

As I hit the ground I turned my head. I don't know why I did, but it saved my face from being crushed into the ground. Then I blacked out, but not for long. I remember getting to my feet and standing a few seconds until my friends laid me back on the ground. I was worried about having a broken back because it hurt. It was hard to breathe. I remember thinking that when people die they usually say, "Well, this is it." I didn't think "this is it," but I was sure that dirt and gravel were in my lungs because it was so hard for me to breathe.

I was taken to the tiny Nye Valley hospital where I was the only patient they had that day. Luckily there was a doctor on call. He and the staff cleaned me off, sewed up my cuts, and told me I had a broken back. I was glad it was nothing more serious but felt terrible about not going on to Mammoth Mountain.

Shortly after, two Elders who were passing the hospital came in and gave me a blessing. No one had told them to come. They were just going by the hospital and decided to come in and see if they were needed. The two came up to me and asked if I wanted a blessing. They didn't know then, and neither did I, but I had a ruptured spleen that immediately repaired itself or I would have bled to death. The internist who cared for me later said: "This is a very unusual occurrence—a spleen healing itself. In fact, it is almost unheard of."

The next morning a doctor from my hometown, Provo, Utah, flew in to see me. As soon as he looked at me, he started to give orders, and I was out of that hospital and into a plane in a hurry.

I don't remember much about the plane ride, but the doctor told me it was a nightmare. He said I blacked out completely two times. The pilot wanted to fly above the storm, but the doctor told him to stay at a lower altitude to keep me alive—the plane did not have a supply of oxygen. An ambulance, oxygen, and my dad were waiting at the Provo airport.

After three weeks of pain, discomfort, discouragement, no food—it wouldn't stay down—continuous intravenous feeding, several blood transfusions, being rushed to intensive care and onto an ice bed several times to reduce an extremely high fever, and having my back and side punctured to remove the fluid from my lungs, the doctors decided that the only thing left to do was to operate and remove one of my kidneys to try to stop the infection and bleeding.

Members of our ward and many of our friends and relatives fasted and prayed for my recovery. I had many wonderful blessings from my father and the bishop. We all had faith that everything would be all right. I made it through the operation, but my heart was weakened. We also wondered if the remaining kidney, which was also diseased, would take over.

The next week was spent in the intensive care unit with a heart monitor registering every beat. At one time the monitor stopped. I told the nurses to call my mother and tell her that the machine said I had just died and ask her if she wanted to come and see me.

I can't tell you how often and how sincerely I prayed for little things—that the nurse would find a vein that wouldn't collapse, that I could swallow something that would stay in my stomach, or that my fever would go down without my having to be packed in ice again. These prayers and many others were always answered.

The doctors, three specialists, told me later what was wrong. Besides a broken back, I had three broken ribs that had punctured my lungs. The pressure, the fluid in my lungs and the infection, as well as the drugs they had to give me, had injured my heart. I also had had a ruptured spleen, which was healed after my blessing from the Elders. One badly diseased kidney was removed, and the other one had infection in it. When my folks asked the operating physician if I would make it, he just shook his head and said: "We can hope. His insides were a mess." He and the other specialists told us later that by all medical standards I should have died soon after the accident and many times since.

I stayed in the hospital about two months. I lost fifty pounds and was so dizzy that I couldn't walk without help. I was to have stayed at home and been taught by a tutor. I was determined to go to school, however, and with the help of a good friend I was able to do it.

Within a few months the doctors said I was completely well. In fact, after a final examination by the internist, he brought out a large assortment of charts and papers, held them up in the air, and said: "What can I say? You are okay. There is absolutely nothing wrong with you. Be careful about contact sports—you have only one kidney—but many, many people live to a very old age with only one kidney. In fact, some people are born with only one. Come back and see me in a year."

I am grateful to be alive and well. I can do anything I ever did before—ski, play tennis, play basketball, exercise. I am so thankful for dedicated doctors, for wonderful, patient nurses, and for well-equipped hospitals; but most of all I thank my Father in Heaven for his many blessings. I'm especially grateful for the opportunity I later had to serve the Lord in the Canada Calgary Mission. I know our Father loves and guides us and that he has a mission for each of his children. He does preserve lives for a purpose greater than we realize.

$\mathscr{P}$lease Help Me Win First Place

BRAD WILCOX

It was the Western Regionals of the *Reader's Digest* Boy Scouts of America National Public Speaking Contest. I rubbed my sweating palms up and down on my pant leg. My number was called. It was my turn to speak.

I stood and smiled calmly. Inside I frantically prayed. *This is it, God. Help me to win it.* Slowly I walked to the front of the auditorium and positioned myself.

As I waited for the timekeeper's signal I surveyed the large audience. Everyone's attention was riveted on me. Again I smiled. Under my controlled facade my legs were shaking like jackhammers. I saw my family, each one beaming. My father winked a "good luck." But I wasn't depending on luck. I had worked. I deserved this. Today was the big day, the moment I would qualify for the national contest in Washington, D.C. My family had come with me all the way to San Francisco for this very moment. *I'm not going to let them down,* I assured myself.

The timer flashed the card and I began my well-rehearsed speech. It flowed simply and naturally. Words leapt from mind to mouth. The audience was with me completely. They listened and laughed exactly in the right places. The final minute ticked off the timer's stopwatch and I built to my triumphant last line. "I explored within and discovered"—I paused—"me."

Applause rang through the auditorium. I walked confidently to my seat. *That's the best I've ever done it,* I thought. The excitement of victory was already racing through my whole body. My face was flushed. I listened to subsequent contestants only enough to feel secure in the knowledge that I had done better than they. Otherwise I sat there trying out dreams of the all-expense trip. I could see myself already on the steps of the White House, Washington, D.C. Wow! I had worked hard, I had earned it, and now I knew it was mine.

After a short lunch break the judges made their decision. Everyone began to file back into the seats. The master of ceremonies gave his thank-you-to-everyone-and-all-the-contestants-were-great speech and started to announce the awards. "Sixth place. . . ." *Thank you, Heavenly Father,* I prayed. *Thank you for helping me win.*

"Third place. . . ." While I was thinking of what I might say when I accepted the trophy, loudly and clearly I heard, "Second place, Brad Wilcox." The words burned through me like a laser beam.

Mom nudged my arm. I stood slowly and walked, zombie-like, to the stage, where I accepted the certificate and took my place with the others.

"Congratulations," the girl next to me offered. I just nodded. I couldn't make a sound come. Second place? Why? Didn't I have the best speech? This wasn't right!

I glared at the words on my certificate—"second place." Heavenly Father had neither heard nor answered my prayer. I bit my lip defiantly. I had done all I could do. I had really tried and he had let me down. Right then on that stage, wallowing in self-pity and hurt pride, I decided, *Trying and prayer don't mix.*

It took me days and weeks to get over the disappointment I felt. I realize now—based on ten specific "steps of trying" that I later formulated—that I had done everything wrong from step one on. But at the time I couldn't see that. I only knew that if Heavenly Father wasn't going to answer my prayers I wouldn't pray; so I didn't.

Then one day in the library during English I read Mark Twain's explanation of this trap, in his story "The War Prayer." The story is about a country at war. The setting is a small town the day before the battalions leave for the front. The church is full of people, all praying for their country's victory.

In Twain's unique way, the story continues with a heavenly messenger entering the church and quietly moving up the main aisle. The messenger proceeds to explain that "as you pray for the blessing of rain upon your crop, you may be working a curse upon your brother's crop that does not need rain and could be injured by it." Noting the bewilderment of the congregation, he puts it even more clearly. "When we pray for our victory we are praying for another's defeat." While that congregation prayed for the lives of their sons, they were offering unspoken prayers that the people they were fighting would lose, and that the enemy would lie dead, murdered; that widows and orphans would wander homeless, hungry and cold through their then-desolated wasteland. This they prayed with humble hearts in "the spirit of love of Him who is the source of love. . . ."

Even after it was put so plainly, the congregation dismissed Mark Twain's messenger as a lunatic "because there was no sense in what he said." I closed the book. *How foolish these people were,* I thought. *Can't they see that simple truth?* Then I thought of myself. My face reddened as I realized how foolish I was being. Each time I pray to win a trophy, win the office, or win the game, I am also offering an unspoken prayer for someone else's defeat.

"Please help me win first place." How selfish I had been in San Francisco. It would have been so much wiser to ask for the strength and determination to earn it. As I was trying I was forgetting to put myself in the shoes of others. Every other contestant too had worked hard and wanted that trip as much as I did. How did I know that every other contestant had not also been praying, and how did I know that the one who won the first place trophy had not worked and prayed harder than any of us?

Rather than stepping on others as I climb, I must honestly help others. After all, wouldn't heaven be a lonely place with only Heavenly Father and me? It's human nature to pray for victory. But wouldn't it be better to pray, instead, to do my best?

Someone to Eat Lunch With

RANDALL C. BIRD

Shortly after we moved to Utah, I noticed that my junior-high-aged daughter was having great fears as her first day of school approached. Many concerns occupied her mind. Who would be her friends? How would she do at a new school? And of course the big question, Who would she sit by during lunch? She had the great fear that by ninth grade everyone would have their group of friends, leaving no space for a move-in and thus leaving her all alone in some corner holding her lunch tray. She prayed daily for two weeks prior to school starting that someone would ask her to eat lunch with them.

Well, the first day of school arrived and she left for the unexpected. How grateful she was when a girl seated behind her in one of her morning classes tapped her on the shoulder and said, "Hey, would you like to eat lunch with me and my friends?"

She came home from that first day of school excited and relieved and with a stronger testimony of the power of prayer. This group of girls had helped her belong. She was now a part of that school and had some friends to associate with.

Saying Prayers

JACK R. CHRISTIANSON

So often we are good at saying prayers but not so good at praying. Sometimes we are so caught up in repeating familiar phrases and using "vain repetitions" that we forget to really talk to our Father. Perhaps the sharing of a little story can illustrate this point.

Two young brothers were arrested one Saturday night for vandalizing an old vacant home. The arresting officer knew they were not bad boys but wanted to scare them a little in hopes that he might teach them a valuable lesson in their young lives. He took them to jail in handcuffs, booked them, and fingerprinted them. After this rough treatment, the boys were terrified and had vowed in their hearts never to do anything wrong again.

The officer was quite pleased with his teaching. When he felt that he had taught the lesson well enough, he phoned the boys' father, explained everything, and asked him to come and pick up the boys. Their father responded with a question: "Can you legally keep them in jail for twenty-four hours?"

"Well, sure," responded the officer. "But they've learned their lesson and are ready to go home now."

The father interjected, "If you can keep them in jail for twenty-four hours, I would like you to do so."

"But, sir. You don't understand. I've already scared them to death, and I'm sure you won't have a problem with them in the future."

Emphatically the father insisted: "If you can legally keep them, I want them to stay!"

"Sir?" the officer asked. "Aren't you a Mormon?"

"Yes," was the reply.

"Don't you want your boys in church tomorrow morning?"

"No! I want them in jail so they can really learn a lesson."

The officer couldn't believe it, and neither could the two brothers.

The next morning when the officer took them breakfast, he stopped and listened as they discussed their dad having left them in jail all night long.

"I can't believe it!" the older boy muttered. "He left us all night!"

"Yeah," responded the younger of the two. "I've never felt bad about missing church until someone told me I couldn't go."

Looking at his watch, the older one said, "We've already missed priesthood meeting, and Sunday School will start in five minutes."

The younger brother then came up with a grand idea: "Why don't we have our own Sunday School. I'll pray if you'll give us a lesson."

The older brother agreed. The officer continued to watch and listen, still holding their plates of food. Then the younger brother began to pray the only way he knew how: "Dear Heavenly Father. We're so grateful that we could all be here today. We're grateful for this beautiful building we have to meet in." And then the kicker. "Please bless all those that aren't with us this week, that they will be with us next week!"

$\mathscr{A}$ Blessing for the Station Wagon

PAULA THOMAS

One afternoon while preparing to teach a lesson I ran across a scripture in Isaiah (Isaiah 61:3) that caused my mind to flood with thoughts on how well Heavenly Father knows his children (you and me). He knew that our human nature could easily fall to the negative side of our earthly experiences, and he told us that in this verse. Isaiah was prophesying about the coming of the Messiah and what his coming would mean to us as God's children. The Messiah would come "to give unto them beauty for ashes, the oil of joy for mourning, the garment of praise for the spirit of heaviness; that they might be called trees of righteousness [children of God]."

Along with Christ's coming to atone for our sins, he would show us by his example that our freedom of choice, or agency, is not just the right to choose between good and evil but also the right to choose every minute of every day how we will respond to life's experiences and to the people who share those experiences with us. The life of Jesus was a constant example of choosing the higher ground.

One of the gifts that Isaiah indicates the Messiah would bring is the "oil of joy for mourning." How does this apply to you and me? There are different levels of mourning. Many of us have lost a loved one who suffered from a disease or encountered a fatal accident. Others of us have suffered or mourned over problems that seemed at the time to have no solution—we have felt despair. I believe that in these most painful hours come our sweetest experiences with a Father in Heaven who is aware of our pain.

Years ago my husband and I loaded up our old green Ford station wagon with a cooler full of food and our four small children and headed for Grand Junction, Colorado. It was a joyful occasion because our sweetest friends had just been baptized members of the Church. We were there to celebrate. After we had rejoiced with them for a couple of days, it was time for us to head home. Because of our financial situation at the time, we referred to trips such as this one as "wing and prayer" trips. We never had quite enough money to make any trip feel too safe.

On this occasion we put our last ten dollars into our gas tank and headed for home. We were about midway between Grand Junction and Salt Lake City on a desolate stretch of freeway when our green station wagon began making a very interesting noise and black smoke started working its way out from under the hood. My husband pulled out of the traffic lane onto the emergency strip. I saw on his face total fear and desperation, because he was not a mechanic. If something was wrong with our car we were going to be very stranded.

There was very little traffic on the freeway that afternoon, so we backed the car up to an exit sign a few yards back from where we had stopped. Along with the exit sign was a sign that read "Services." The word had been crossed out. We followed the exit road down to an old gas station that was all boarded up. My husband turned the engine off, and we all sat in silence.

Our children, even though they were very young, were intuitively aware of the anxiety that hovered in the car. My husband, Dave, got out of the car and looked under the hood, hoping that something would leap to his attention that he would be able to fix with his limited knowledge of mechanics. He saw nothing but leftover black smoke. We were in trouble. Our hearts were heavy with the desperation of the moment. As parents we were mourning the circumstances we had placed our little family in by undertaking a "wing and prayer" adventure.

As we all sat in silence, a little voice from the back of the car said, "Dad, can't you give our car a blessing and make it better, just like you do with people?" We turned to look at our six-year-old son, Jim. His eyes were full of confidence that his suggestion would work. It was as if he couldn't figure out why we hadn't thought of it.

A very teachable father followed the counsel of an inspired six-year-old and said, "I think first we all need to pray together; then I will go out and bless our car." We offered a prayer; then Dave went out to the front of the car. He shut the hood and gently placed his hands on our only way home. Four little sets of eyes looked on without a doubt in their minds that, with the priesthood, Dad was going to heal their green station wagon. Dave gave the car a sweet and gentle blessing, then returned to the driver's seat to turn on the ignition.

As the engine started we waited to see if the black smoke was still our companion. No smoke came. We returned to the freeway to finish off the last leg of our adventure.

We felt so lost and alone as we sat in front of that skeleton of a station, but in the darkest of moments came a loving Father in Heaven to offer us the "oil of joy," to show us his hand in our lives—to heal even a car.

We had been home for two days when the black smoke and the noise came again. We had, as mechanics would say, thrown a rod. The repair was so big that the car was not worth fixing.

I know there are people in this world who would say that this experience was just plain luck; or maybe that the car was not in that bad a shape. Some of you might say that kind of thing never happens to you. Maybe you feel that you have never had a prayer answered, or you think you've never had a spiritual experience. Isaiah was saying to you and me that we need to open our eyes a little wider, rely a little more on our spirit, listen a little more intently to the still, small voice within us so that we can see God's hand in our lives—so we can see the light. I feel that if God knows that we are watching more carefully and listening a little harder, he will give us moments of enlightenment that reveal the miracles in simple things.

$\mathscr{A}$ Still Small Voice

WAYNE B. LYNN

Only a fool or a fisherman would be up at this early hour, and as I reflected upon it, I wasn't sure there was a great deal of difference between the two.

It was 3:00 A.M. on a cold winter morning. The month was February, and the place was northern Wyoming, where I was teaching school in a lovely little town called Byron. Not too far west from where we lived was the Shoshone Reservoir, more commonly called the Buffalo Bill Dam. It was located near Cody, Wyoming, next to the highway leading toward the east entrance to Yellowstone Park. This was great fishing country, and a little cold weather didn't bother us natives at all. Reports of other successes were sufficient to get us out of our warm beds on this cold Saturday morning. My father arrived at my home and put our lunches and fishing gear into my car while I scraped frost off the windshield. The stars were winking brightly and the cold air was sweet and crisp. Before leaving the house we paused for a moment and kneeled together in prayer to ask for the Lord's protection and for his Spirit to guide us through the day. Two more stops and we would be on our way. Our first stop was for my friend Rick. When our lights beamed into his driveway he was alerted to our arrival. Dressed like an Eskimo, he appeared immediately at the door with a large iron bar in hand that I had recently transformed into an ice pick for him. A hearty greeting, a loading of gear, and then on to our last stop at a small stream of water flowing from a natural spring nearby. This was where we kept our live minnows.

The car soon warmed up as we began our fifty-mile journey

to the lake. We loosened our heavy clothing, not wanting to get too warm. The conversation was animated even at this early hour as thoughts of the big ones filled our imaginations. Mackinaw, rainbows, and browns were all biting, and winter trout is as delicious as anything you can name.

We were racing daybreak because early hours seemed to be the best time to fish.

Two rivers flow into the huge lake we were headed for: the North Fork of the Shoshone River and the South Fork. Fish often gather where the rivers flow into the lake. They lie in wait facing upstream as their food supply floats down the current from the river.

We decided on fishing the South Fork side of the lake, so we took the left turn at the highway junction a few miles west of Cody. It was still dark when we parked the car and bundled up for our foray out upon the frozen surface. The lake shone like a huge sparkling jewel in the moonlight. Loaded with gear, we wended our way down the slope for nearly a hundred yards to reach the sandy beach and edge of the lake. Pieces of driftwood and melted snowbanks marked the crooked shoreline. We took our first steps upon the slippery surface with some trepidation as we cautiously moved out on the ice.

As we took those first few steps, a strong feeling of apprehension flooded over me, and I noted that my father had a similar impression.

"Let's just fish right here," my father suggested.

"No way, they're biting out where the river feeds in," was Rick's rebuttal. "We'll never catch anything here."

"This ice scares me," Dad said. "Somehow I don't trust it. Let's just give it a try here near the shore."

"Here, let me show you," Rick countered, and he began chipping into the icy surface with his sharp new ice pick. In a moment he had chopped a hole over fifteen inches deep and was still going strong. "This would hold up a truck," was his comment, and he was right. But our destination was about one-half mile out on the ice, and that's a long, risky way to go from shore.

We disregarded our apprehensions and moved out onto the lake, but the nagging feeling persisted—not one of logic but just a gut-level feeling that we "hadn't oughta."

We were among the first to arrive at our predetermined spot. We were not alone, but the lake was so huge that the parties were widely separated in relative isolation.

Let me explain a few of the technical aspects of this sort of fishing. Most parties carry an old iron bucket filled with ashes and soaked with kerosene. This can be torched and, with an occasional stirring, will burn the entire morning to help keep us warm.

The air was so cold that morning we could hear voices from across the lake as clearly as if the people were standing next to us. The movement of the water underneath the expanding ice caused it to creak and crack and give off constant groanings and rifle-like retorts.

We had trudged across the vast ice and found our way up near the south confluence, having crossed over the lake from the east side. Now, with our fire lit for warmth, we proceeded to dig several fishing holes. The heavy rod we used for an ice pick was made from an old car axle to which I had welded a piece of leaf spring. This spring was cut to form three long teeth, each sharpened to a point. Ice would really fly, and a hole in the eighteen-inch-thick ice could be carved out in a few minutes. The round holes we chopped were about eighteen to twenty inches in diameter. As we chopped, we scooped out the ice chips, being careful not to penetrate through to the water until the hole was nearly complete.

Once the hole was chopped we rigged our poles. Fish-and-game laws require the use of a fish pole, but we actually land the fish by raising the line hand over hand. Fish poles are useless here because the eyelets soon freeze solid.

We fastened a large hook to several feet of leader that was tied to the line. About eighteen inches above the hook we placed a relatively heavy bell sinker, heavy enough to carry hook and bait to the bottom. Next, we pushed the hook through the back of a live minnow for bait and lowered him and the weight into the cold green water. We let out the line hand over hand until we felt the weight strike bottom; then we lifted the line about two feet off the lake bottom and fastened a brightly colored red-and-white bobber to the line at water level. We were allowed only one line each, but we helped watch each other's lines.

When the bobber started sinking or bobbing up and down, our hearts would go up and down with it! We knew what was on the other end! A skillful pause as the bobber sank, then a quick jerk on the line to set the hook—and the fun started! The beautiful trout we pulled splashing and twisting to the surface weighed one or two pounds each.

Landing a fish every few minutes, we soon found ourselves totally absorbed in this fantastic sport. One huge German brown trout gave us a real run for our money. When he was finally landed we estimated his weight as four pounds. Rick had landed him and in his exuberance yelled, "Oh, shucks, he's just a brown. Let's kick him back in!" As he spoke he gave a fake kick toward the fish and the hole in the ice. The fish chose that very moment to leap in the air, and before Rick could pull back his foot, he had kicked him directly back into the hole. Mr. Brown promptly made a lifesaving exit into the deep waters. All was quiet for a minute and then we broke into laughter. It was the biggest fish we had caught all day, and we had kicked him back down the hole! It was too funny for words.

Things quieted down a little after that as we continued fishing. By this time, the sun had risen and was shining brightly. We had even shed our heavy coats. We had recently had a few nice days like this when the weather suddenly turned unseasonably warm.

My attention was turned toward my father, who was in the process of catching a fish, when an overpowering sense of urgency flooded through my body. Looking over at my father I spoke with a feeling of near alarm: "Dad, I think we need to get out of here right now." Without argument my dad replied, "I think so too; let's do it." To my amazement, he pulled his line away from a sure catch and began gathering up his gear. Rick looked at us strangely but didn't argue. We nearly had our limit anyway.

With a heavy string of fish in one hand and my fish pole and gear box in the other, I led our trio in the trek back over the lake. Our sense of urgency persisted, so I walked quickly. With my attention focused ahead I was totally surprised when, without warning, the ice under my feet gave way, and I found myself immersed in icy waters to my armpits. My outthrown arms kept me from submerging further. I gave a loud cry in reaction to the cold and the surprise, and as quickly as I could I managed to lift myself out of the hole and onto firmer footing. Quick observation revealed that the ice had formed into small, narrow crystals in a honeycomb pattern. Even though the ice was thick, it would not support my weight but allowed my feet to push through into the frigid water.

Getting back to my feet, I ventured forward again more cautiously. I had traveled perhaps twenty yards when I fell through again. Again I climbed out, and as I did, the shore seemed a mighty long distance away. In reality it was nearly half a mile. Again we ventured forward, and this time when I fell through it became more serious. As I tried to extricate myself, the ice broke off and refused to support my weight. The hole became larger and larger; it was as big as an automobile before I finally found ice strong enough to allow me to climb out.

It was decided that perhaps my father should lead out, since he didn't weigh as much as I did. As serious as things looked, we all laughed when he fell through. He gave a loud, "Hooo! this water's cold!" Rick was next to lead us, being the smallest of the three; however, he soon fell through and, like me, could not find ice to support himself. I noted with alarm that he was beginning to panic, and he had a wild, glazed look in his eyes. As carefully as I could, I crawled over to him on my stomach and extended a helping hand. Our fingers finally touched, and I dragged him nearly exhausted out upon the ice. When he recovered slightly, he rose to his feet and started almost running toward shore. He succeeded in going nearly one hundred yards without incident.

Pausing briefly, he turned back toward us and yelled, "If you make it out to here I think you'll be all right!" Having said this, he turned, took a few steps, and promptly fell through the ice.

Our return was a nightmare. We soon realized that if we had tarried even a few minutes longer, we would have had a cold, watery grave. As it turned out, we struggled closer and closer to the distant shore. As we walked, we searched for the right-colored ice or stronger snowpack, but it was totally unpredictable. We never knew when we would suddenly sink into the frigid waters of the lake.

We shouted warnings to other fishermen who were closer to shore. They saw our predicament and scampered to safety. In a true act of cowardice and lack of consideration, they packed their gear and left, leaving us in our circumstances although our warning shouts had literally saved them.

I can't say we were truly frightened until we drew within about one hundred yards from shore. By now, we had fallen in numerous times but had persistently pressed forward. With each step we took, the surface of the ice would ripple like a blanket many yards ahead. It looked as though the entire ice cap was about to disintegrate. Both the ice and the temperature would have made swimming to safety impossible.

At last Rick somehow reached the shore and managed to build a fire from driftwood. A game warden had parked his truck by my car and had joined Rick. They were both intently watching our progress.

It is hard to describe our feelings when our feet finally touched the solid shore at almost the same instant. We looked back over our tortuous path marked by holes and water. Without question, even a few minutes delay in leaving our first position would have meant certain tragedy. We were distracted for a moment from our reverie by an insensitive game warden who seemed more concerned with seeing our fishing licenses than enquiring about our physical well-being. As we warmed ourselves around the fire, our thoughts returned to those early-morning hours when we first stepped out upon the ice and to the warning "feeling" that we had both disregarded. This had all happened only a few hours before, but it seemed like ages ago. Although we had failed to heed the Lord's warning, he had given us another chance and had warned us again. This time we had listened. I recalled as I turned to warm myself in front of the fire how we had knelt at home that morning and asked the Lord for guidance. Yet we had disregarded the guidance when it was given. My thoughts turned to Nephi of old as he scolded his older brothers: "He hath spoken unto you in a still small voice, but ye were past feeling, that ye could not feel his words" (1 Nephi 17:45).

The Lord had almost shouted in our ears, and we listened and were saved. We joshed each other on the way home; it was a way of relieving tension. Rick said little. He was embarrassed at his own behavior.

I was complimented on how fresh I had kept the fish. I had held them tightly in my hand, and only after we reached safety ashore had I become consciously aware of them once again.

I had dunked them frequently in cold water. Unfortunately, I was dunked along with them. That night I knelt on the same living-room carpet. This time my prayer was one of sincere thanksgiving. It was also a prayer of resolve that I would try to live so as to merit the promptings of "that still small voice" and to be prepared to hear and feel it when it came. I prayed for faith and courage to act upon those divine impressions.

The fish were delicious, and you might also safely say that it was a fishing trip we would not soon forget.

Attitude
and
Self-Worth

$\mathcal{You}$ Choose Your Attitude

SHANE BARKER

When I was on my mission, I had a companion named Elder Bonham. He was the most friendly, outgoing, optimistic, full-of-energy-and-ready-to-baptize Elder I had ever known. Living with him was like living with a bottle rocket. Even on the hardest, most miserable days, his high-voltage personality kept things bright and cheery.

I admired him for that. And I wished that I could be just like him.

And then I realized that I *could* be. Elder Bonham didn't do anything that I couldn't do. After all, *I* could be happy. *I* could be optimistic. *I* could be energetic.

The moment I realized that, my mission changed. Every morning I got up trying to be as happy as I could. I tried to look for the bright side of things. I tried to be upbeat and optimistic.

It wasn't always easy. But the more I worked at it, the easier it became. And every night and morning, when I said my personal prayers, I asked for help in keeping it up.

And what a difference it made! I felt like a new person. I charged into my work with more energy than ever before.

Whatever attitude you have, it's one that *you* choose. You have the power to maintain a happy outlook on life. You can charge the batteries and energize the lives of the people around you. That alone will make you stand out among your friends.

But it will make your own life more fun, too.

Why Don't You Look at the Sky?

GEORGE D. DURRANT

I recall the first art class I took, way back in my early college days. It took all the confidence I could muster just to enroll. I knew that everyone else in the class would be Leonardo da Vincis and I'd suffer much self-inflicted humiliation as I compared my meager abilities with theirs.

I did my first painting for the class in watercolors. It turned out a little better than I thought it might when I first put the paint on the paper. Even so, I was shocked and filled with fear when the teacher announced, "I see that most of you have completed your first painting. So let's all put them up here along the wall. When they are all in place we will criticize one another's work."

I thought to myself, *I didn't know I'd have to put my picture up to be criticized. If I had known that, I would have never taken this class.*

But having no choice, I reluctantly put my picture on the far right of the display. I hoped that the criticism would begin with the pictures on the left side and maybe the class time would end before it was my turn. Or I hoped at least they'd use up all their criticisms on the other paintings before they got to mine.

As the discussions of the first few paintings were taking place, I didn't say anything about anybody else's efforts. I hoped my silence would indicate that I had no desire to criticize their work, and then, if they were Christians, they wouldn't say anything about mine.

But the clock moved so slowly and the discussion so rapidly that with five minutes remaining, all eyes except mine focused on my work. My insecurities made it so that I could not muster the courage to look up. As everyone looked at my painting, there were several seconds of silence.

Then I heard a girl's voice. In a quiet, kindly tone she said, "I like the sky." Those four words gave me a small feeling of confidence. I lifted my eyes and looked up at the painting. To myself I said, *By George, that* is *a nice sky.*

From the other side of the room, a fellow spoke up. "But he has got the foreground all fouled up."

In my mind I responded, *Why don't you look at the sky?*

And then I thought, *Next time he won't be able to say such a thing, because next time my foreground will be as good as my sky.*

So now, many years after that experience, I say to all of you and to myself what I said then: Why don't *we* look at the sky— and then go to work and beautify our foreground so it will be like our sky.

To you whose foreground is colored with muddy gray meanness, I say: Look up at the sky and see what you ought to be, what you could be. Then begin to paint into your foreground some bright-colored kindness. As you do so, you'll be headed toward happiness.

To you whose habits and behavior are degrading, I say: Look up and see the purity of the true blue of your sky. Paint your foreground with colors that will show your loyalty to your family, to God, and to yourself. Then you'll see a road sign saying Happiness This Way.

To you whose foreground is painted with the drab colors of discouragement and despair, I say: Look up to the light of the sky and see the hope there. Paint yourself some new goals, goals that will lead you through the density of a self-pitying foreground and onto the path of hope.

To you who have painted your foreground with thick jungles of sins that cling to you like the snags of life's thistles, I say: Look up. An upward gaze will give you the desire to wipe life's paper clean and to begin to paint a path that will get you through to a happier place.

Looking up at the sky can symbolize seeing and loving the

good, and seeing and loving God. When we see the good in ourselves and in others, we will see the direction that will move us ever closer to that which matters most—happiness.

$\mathcal{R}$ehearsing Success

SUZANNE L. HANSEN

Winners always picture or visualize themselves accomplishing their goals. But in the face of hard times it's a little more difficult for some to see opportunity and success—as Davy Hair did.

On Father's Day 1978 this brawny eighteen-year-old was working as a lifeguard at a swimming pool in Fairfield, New Jersey. Suddenly, amidst the fun-filled sounds of swimming children, came a shrill cry for help.

Davy's heart started to pound in anticipation. He looked quickly around and spotted a child struggling in the deep end and crying for help. Davy reacted quickly and dived off the nine-foot lifeguard stand into the pool.

The next thing Davy saw was a white flash as his head struck the concrete bottom of the pool. The water turned red around him, and Davy felt himself starting to slip away. Then he felt someone pull him to the surface. It was his brother, Brian.

Davy muttered over and over, "There's someone in trouble, there's someone in trouble." "Don't worry," Brian said. And then came those penetrating words: "The kid was faking it."

Davy's neck was broken. He had irreversible spinal damage. He was paralyzed. The next day Davy spent three hours in surgery. The doctors rebuilt his shattered neck, taking bone from his hip to do so.

"Let me die," became Davy's cry. He had had everything before. Six-foot-four, 220 pounds, blonde hair, blue eyes, a leader, tons of friends, a passion for sports and a love of life— now flat on his back, unable even to feed himself. What did life have to offer?

Davy thought of suicide, but he wasn't even capable of doing that. Then one day he looked at his loving family, who were continually by his side. He looked at his brother, Brian, who had saved his life and who kept telling Davy that he could beat this. Davy decided then that he owed it to them to at least give life a try. With that decision he had started on the road of winning from within.

After many months in the hospital and many difficult therapy sessions, Davy had regained the use of his upper body. He announced to his mother: "A wheelchair is not important. I used to walk from one place to another. Now I go on wheels. What's important is what I do when I get there."

Six months after the accident Davy moved home and started school again. He began swimming and lifting weights. One of his teachers suggested he enter wheelchair track events. He pictured himself entering races and winning, and hurling the shot long distances. But disappointment after disappointment came. However, he did not give up.

In 1979 Davy won a bronze medal in the shot put at a wheelchair track event. There he met the world champion wheelchair athlete, whose muscular chest and arms and powerful throws astonished him.

Davy made up his mind that he was going to beat that guy. Over and over in his mind he rehearsed pulling up to the mark and hurling way beyond the champion's throw. He even saw the crowd going crazy.

Davy's training now began in earnest. At seven o'clock each morning Brian helped him stretch his arms. Afterwards he swam half a mile and then worked out for two hours on a weight-training machine over his bed. With this strenuous regime he increased his strength till he was able to bench-press four hundred pounds and his biceps bulged to eighteen and a half inches. In 1982 Davy won three gold medals at the World Games, beating the champion. The moment he had rehearsed in his mind for three years had happened. In 1985 he graduated from law school and picked up three more gold medals at the National Wheelchair Games.

Davy occasionally recalls those days of despair in the hospital. "I remember thinking," he says, "that one day I would stand at the gates of heaven and God would ask what I did with my life. And I would respond that I broke my neck, so I didn't have to do anything."

Sure, the neck could have become an excuse. But Davy stopped concentrating on what he couldn't do and rehearsed over and over in his mind success and winning. And that's what happened.

They Say

VAL C. WILCOX

What will they think if I should dare
To choose and buy this one to wear?

They say it simply can't be done,
No point in even trying one.

I might compete and then just see—
But if I fail they'll laugh at me.

Though sometimes many, sometimes few,
It seems *they* dictate all I do.

The only thing they do not say
Is just exactly who are they!

$\mathscr{T}$he Eighty Percent

BARBARA BARRINGTON JONES

When my husband, Hal, and I were first married, he said: "There's eighty percent of me that's good and there's twenty percent of me that is not so good. If you choose to look at my eighty percent, we are going to be happy. If you choose to look at my twenty percent, our marriage isn't going to be all that great." So it is with many things in our lives.

Most parents have eighty percent that is good and twenty percent that's not so good. The same is true of brothers, sisters, school, work, and even many of the experiences we have in church. It is up to us to decide which part to look at—the eighty or the twenty. In any person or situation, we can choose to dwell on either the negative or the positive. And just as my husband says, we can all find greater happiness if we look for the eighty.

My daughter, Wendy, had a rough junior year in high school. Looking back on it she says, "Mom, it was all because of my own attitude."

I remember taking her to a beauty shop before school started, because she wanted a new hairstyle. When the cut was done, Wendy turned to me with tears in her eyes and cried: "I hate it! You've ruined me!"

After the first day of school, I picked Wendy up. Before she even got in the car she said: "Mom, this is going to be the worst year of my entire life. Do you know who I got for my classes? Do you know who's in my classes?" She then complained about each teacher and student throughout her entire schedule.

I thought, *In a few days this will all blow over.* I was wrong.

You see, Wendy liked one guy, but he never asked her out. Then another guy started asking her out, and he was okay but he wasn't as good as the first guy. When Christmas came, neither guy asked her to the formal because they both thought the other one already had. Wendy didn't get to go at all. "I told you this would be the worst year," she sobbed.

I said, "Wendy, look for the eighty percent."

"You sound just like Dad!" she wailed.

Soon after this, Wendy's good friends Jason and Andy were traveling to a game where Wendy was cheerleading. They were involved in a terrible car accident and were both killed. "It was a horrible accident," the papers reported. "It's so sad," teachers and friends said. "It should never have happened," was the comment heard over and over at school. But, like many difficult and trying circumstances of life, it did happen. None of us had control over that. We couldn't change it.

Wendy was devastated by the deaths. She was upset and angry. She was mad at the situation and the world; and deep down, she was mad at God. Rather than lifting an open hand upward for Heavenly Father's help when she needed it most, Wendy chose instead to raise a fist.

As the year came to an end, Wendy decided, at her dad's suggestion, that it would be healthy to get away. She signed up with Teen Missions International, a youth service group that was going to New Guinea to do work projects for the needy.

After two days of training, Wendy and her group flew to Australia and then to New Guinea. There they were loaded in the back of trucks and driven for forty-eight hours to the edge of a river. The group was then put in canoes for an eighteen-hour trip to the village where they would live. By that time these young people were exhausted. They had jet lag, truck lag, and canoe lag. They wanted to crash in bed and sleep, but the only thing they were given were sleeping bags and tents.

Most of the time, it was pouring with rain. It was also very hot—one hundred twenty degrees, to be exact. The only type of shoes that the young people could bring were a pair of work boots, and in the weeks that followed, those boots were worn out completely.

Wendy's work team built a hospital and a bridge. They had no machinery, so everything had to be done by hand. Wendy worked harder than she ever had. The team awoke early and rarely even stopped for a rest during the day. They couldn't. If they didn't get their part of the construction done on time it would hold up other groups.

Wendy recalls: "At night I wanted to cry, but no tears ever came. I had blisters that were sore and broken. My back hurt and my muscles ached. I wanted to cry, but it was too hard." So it went, day after day, until one afternoon, while timbers for the bridge were being moved, an accident occurred. A huge log fell and crushed the hand of one of the team members. The girl screamed in pain. Blood was everywhere.

Quickly the group gathered around and hoisted the heavy wood off their friend's hand. Adult supervisors called on short-wave radio for a helicopter to come, and the injured girl was flown out for medical help.

The teenagers who remained behind were tired. These young people were sore, dirty, and covered with sweat. They could have said: "This is stupid! We want to go home. If we weren't here in this awful place, this accident never would have happened." The teenagers could have complained loud and long about their supervisors, their companions, and their horrible accommodations. They could have said, "This has been the worst experience of our lives."

However, these teenagers chose a different course. They looked for the eighty. In their anxiety and total helplessness, these teenagers did not gripe and whine. Rather, they knelt in prayer. They prayed over and over into the night.

Finally, at 3:00 A.M., the team got a call that their friend would be O.K. In fact, not one bone in the girl's hand had been broken.

Wendy says: "That's when I cried—not because of my troubles and problems, but out of gratitude." Yes, this time there were tears—not of self-pity but of appreciation. Prayers had been answered. Lives had been changed. Wendy felt as if she had witnessed a miracle.

When my daughter finally came home I was waiting as she got off the plane. She looked like a native of New Guinea. She had on a long muumuu and was even carrying spears. She was tanned and exhausted, but she was smiling and laughing. Handing her spears to one of her teammates, and signaling for me to wait, she whipped off her muumuu. Underneath, she had on a nice skirt and top that she had bought in Australia. She looked fantastic. She was healthy, in shape, and feeling great.

I asked, "What do you want to do first?"

"I want to take a real bath," she answered. When we got home and Wendy turned on the water she exclaimed, "Look, Mom, running water!" In the days that followed, Wendy couldn't stop counting her blessings. Suddenly she was seeing all the good things in her life. She had gained a testimony that God lives, loves us, and really is there for us—even during hard times. Wendy looked for the eighty and, at last, she found it.

At the start of her senior year, Wendy went to the hairdresser—the same one she had gone to the previous year. After the cut, Wendy looked in the mirror and said: "I love it. I just love it, and I love you too!" The hairdresser almost fainted. My daughter had a wonderful senior year. The teachers were the same as the year before. The students were the same. The school had not really changed at all. But—and here's the point—Wendy's attitude had.

You Can Be a Hero

SHANE BARKER

You don't have to have the body of a beauty queen for people to admire you. You don't have to be a superman with rippling muscles to become a hero.

Let me give you an example.

I used to coach a Little League baseball team. One morning we were playing the best team in the league. We were in the middle of a losing streak, and we weren't just expected to lose. We were expected to get killed.

But we played our hearts out, and by the last inning we were behind by a single run. With two outs, we had runners on second and third. All we needed was a base hit to win the game.

The only problem was that Steve McClaren was up to bat.

Now, Steve was one of my favorite players. He was a good right fielder, and he had a sense of humor that kept everyone happy—even when we were down by a dozen runs or so. But he was the worst hitter on the team.

I tried to be optimistic as he dug himself into the batter's box. "C'mon, Steve," I shouted. "Base hit wins the game, bud! Be a hitter, now!"

Steve took a couple of practice swings, then leaned over the plate.

"You can do it, Steve!" I shouted. "Give it a ride, now! Smack it out of here!"

Steve stared toward the pitcher. The ball came in high and tight . . . a tough pitch to hit.

Steve swung anyway.

And smacked the ball past the shortstop!

He bolted for first as both base runners charged home. The umpire held his mask in the air.

We'd won the game!

The team exploded from the dugout, swarming onto the field and piling on Steve like they'd just won the World Series.

I couldn't believe it. We'd won! We'd beaten the best team in the league! I was so choked up I couldn't move.

And Steve!

We had good athletes on the team. But Steve was the last person on earth I would have picked to win the game for us.

But like I said, *anyone* can be a hero.

Even you!

You might never sink the winning shot in a basketball game. You might never rescue a little kid from a burning house. And you might never star in your own music video. But you can be a hero in the life of the most important person in the world. You!

You become the hero of your own life story by reaching difficult goals. Doing things you thought you were too scared to try. Reaching new heights. Pushing yourself to your fullest potential.

You do it by daring to be your very best self.

It Couldn't Be Done

EDGAR A. GUEST

Somebody said that it couldn't be done,
　But he with a chuckle replied
That "maybe it couldn't," but he would be one
　Who wouldn't say so till he'd tried.
So he buckled right in with the trace of a grin
　On his face. If he worried he hid it.
He started to sing as he tackled the thing
　That couldn't be done, and he did it.

Somebody scoffed: "Oh, you'll never do that;
　At least no one ever has done it";
But he took off his coat and he took off his hat,
　And the first thing we knew he'd begun it.
With a lift of his chin and a bit of a grin,
　Without any doubting or quiddit,
He started to sing as he tackled the thing
　That couldn't be done, and he did it.

There are thousands to tell you it cannot be done,
　There are thousands to prophesy failure;
There are thousands to point out to you one by one,
　The dangers that wait to assail you.
But just buckle in with a bit of a grin,
　Just take off your coat and go to it;
Just start in to sing as you tackle the thing
　That "cannot be done," and you'll do it.

"Just One of Those Things"

SUZANNE L. HANSEN

I have a dear friend who has an "I can" attitude. Her outlook on life has inspired me and many others. She has what a lot of people would call problems. But she doesn't see it that way.

Her name is Kathy Vorwaller. She was born with a malformed body. She has no arms at all, and has one leg that is very short and has no knee joint. The other leg is normal, but the foot has only four toes.

Kathy admits that her disability was a mystery. But she really doesn't dwell on it. She says in her matter-of-fact way, "This is just one of those things that happens in life."

The Vorwaller parents treated Kathy as normal to whatever extent was possible, with responsibilities and opportunities like those of their other children. Kathy's mother, Inga, always reminded her that God doesn't make mistakes, that Kathy was born with everything she needed to be successful in life.

Kathy doesn't like to bump her head when she falls, so on the way down she tries to catch herself with her shoulder. This process has resulted in a snapped collarbone seven times. She has also had two broken legs.

But Kathy has made things happen in her life. With an artificial leg attached to her short leg, she conquered public schools, graduating from high school. Determined to enjoy normal activities, she has learned to use her feet as hands. She does needlepoint, types, programs computers, plays chess, and even puts on her own makeup with her toes. And with great zeal and enthusiasm she also rides horseback, camps with her family, water-skis, roller-skates, and dreams of skydiving.

How many of us with all our limbs enjoy and use them so fully for fun and growth?

At the Utah State Fair Kathy has even won the top honor for her stitchery. She graduated from Salt Lake Community College, and today she works for Utah Transit Authority as a computer programmer.

When I asked Kathy how she does it all, she smiled and said, "I just get down on my one knee and thank God every day for my foot that works."

May I Have This Dance?

BRAD WILCOX

All right, all you boys. There are lots of girls who would love to dance, so let's get busy." Our tour adviser looked directly at Jason and me and then turned on the music again. A tropical breeze shuffled through leaves in a planter behind us on the hotel patio.

I had only just finished eighth grade and didn't even know how to dance by myself, let alone ask a girl to do it with me.

"I guess we should go dance, Brad." Jason was rolling up the embroidered sleeves of his I'm-a-tourist-in-Mexico shirt he had bought that afternoon.

"No, not me."

"But Mr. Jarman said there are girls who want to dance, and anyway this is the last night of the tour and we'll probably never see them again." A sudden gust blew Jason's hair across his eyes. Casually he brushed it back again.

This educational tour through Mexico had been sponsored by our school district, and up to now it had been a great experience. Why did they have to spoil it with a dance?

"Come on." Jason got me to my feet. "You ask Joan, and I'll ask Christie." He buttoned his top shirt button, moved across the patio, and offered his hand. "Hey, Christie, would you like to dance?"

I stood back and watched in hopes of gaining instant learning in the intricacies of social interaction.

Christie flipped her hair. "Gee . . . ah . . . thanks, Jason, but not right now."

"What about you, Joan?" he asked.

From my safe position behind the lines, I noticed Jason's crooked-tooth smile. I saw my friend for the first time as those girls might be seeing him, and I guess, overall, he did look kind of unusual.

"I'd really like to dance, Jason, but I don't like this song."

He tugged at his gaudy new shirt. "Well, maybe later?"

The two embarrassed girls looked quickly at each other. "Oh . . . ah . . . we're not feeling too well."

After a moment he came back to me. "Okay, Brad, who should we ask next?"

I still couldn't believe what Joan had said. "Not feeling well!" I complained to Jason. "She felt well enough to dance with Monroe a few minutes ago."

"But he's a senior in high school. We're only eighth graders."

"Ninth grade now," I reminded him. I followed him to the tile fountain in the center of the patio, where Stephanie LeBette stood. With her hand on her hip and her nose in the air, she might as well have been a water-spouting statue.

I realized what Jason was about to do even before he said, "Hey, Stephanie, how about a dance?"

"Jason, don't . . ." I turned away with elaborate casualness. Stephanie broke her pose to smile disdainfully and glide haughtily away.

"Well, how about it, you want to dance?" Jason called after her.

"No, gracias, señor." She didn't even bother to look back.

I pushed a ripple into the fountain pool. "I don't get it, Jas. I thought girls liked to dance."

"They do," he assured me. "Look, why don't *you* ask Stephanie?"

"No way, not her. I don't want to get turned down, too."

With his square fingers Jason jarred the water again, contorting our shadowed reflections.

"Brad, if Stephanie doesn't want to dance it's her problem, not yours."

"But if she said no, why keep asking her?"

"Why not?"

The director turned up the music again. Jason stepped closer to me to be heard. "Why should you let *her* decide how you're going to act?" He touched his greased hair, which was unmoved since the last time. "I'm going over there and ask some new girls. Want to come?"

I shook my head and sat on the tile rim. Even through my thick jeans it felt cold. Jason walked away, stepping awkwardly to the musical beat.

As I think back on the incident, I realize that Jason is one of the few people I've ever known who *acts* toward people. Most of us *react* to people. He knew what he wanted and how he should behave. If Stephanie had refused me like that, I'd have either crawled off and buried myself in a Mexican pyramid or said, "You're not so neat yourself, you goat," and maybe bitten her ankle or something.

I remember that evening as though I were a character in a cartoon sitting by that cold fountain thinking, but with nothing written in my thought bubble. If I were to fill it in now, I guess I'd write, "No one is more miserable than the dummy who always reacts."

At that long-ago dance my center of confidence was outside myself, being kicked around that patio like an old can. If Christie had said, "You're cold," I'd have sneezed. If Monroe had said, "You're hot," I'd have wiped my forehead. My feelings toward the whole situation were totally dependent upon a few people who could decide if I were to be embarrassed or proud, rude or gracious, introverted or extroverted. Unlike Jason, whose emotional security was rooted within himself as it should be, I had relinquished control of my own personality.

I'm thankful for that skinny tourist friend and for the important principle he personified: to act and not to react. For in all the dances I've attended since that bomb-out in Mexico, not once have I bitten Stephanie LeBette's ankle (or even any other girl's).

"Jesus Loves You"

RANDAL A. WRIGHT

When my neighbor Shane was on his mission in Plymouth, England, he was asked to speak in sacrament meeting. Before the meeting started, he went to the back of the chapel to spend some quiet time reviewing his talk. A curly-haired five-year-old boy walked up to him and asked, "What's wrong?" Joking with the little boy, he said, "Nobody loves me, and I don't have any friends. That's why I'm sitting back here by myself." The young boy looked up at him very seriously and said, "Jesus loves you." This young boy already realized that Jesus is our friend and that he loves us.

$\mathcal{H}$ands

STEPHEN JASON HALL

$\mathbf{A}$fter a diving accident that left me paralyzed from the chest down, I spent over a year in and out of different hospitals and therapeutic institutions, during which time I learned some of the valuable lessons of my life. Most important, I found that although none of us has exactly the same adversity as someone else, the ways we overcome are similar and can be applied across the board. I'd like to share one of those ways with you.

I woke up especially early that mid-September morning, for my mind was particularly full. September had been an unusually hard month for me. Three hundred and fifty miles northwest from Salt Lake City, in Boise, all of my classmates had started high school and were enjoying all the joys that accompany it. While they attended football games and pep rallies (not to mention those senior cheerleaders), I was stuck in a hospital waiting for my daily meds. This state of mind easily allowed me to focus on what I didn't have.

I especially concentrated on the paralysis of my hands and all of the things I could not do because of that paralysis. Nightly I would pray that I might regain the use of my hands. It did not seem too much to ask; I figured I had been a good kid, I did not really deserve a crippling handicap. And I became altogether sure that if this partial healing took place I could then be happy. I began to spend all my time concentrating on all the things that I would be able to do if I only had use of this faculty. It seemed such a simple act for a God who created the worlds, and I knew that with the use of my hands I could lead a normal and happy life. In short, I could live as a paraplegic but not as a quadriplegic.

Luckily, even in the face of such an attitude I had resolved that in my daily therapy I would give everything I had. Hours upon hours I exercised, stretching and pulling, doing everything in my power to strengthen my remaining muscles. It was hard, but the time went quickly enough, and my daily progress made it all worth it—until Dan came.

Dan had been in an accident similar to mine and it caused his spine to be damaged and paralysis to ensue. But he had escaped with total use of his hands and partial use of his legs. He was part of a world that I could only dream of joining. Yet he would sit there the entire therapy hour whining and complaining that he was unable to totally use his legs. "Today, let's concentrate on your upper body," the therapist would plead daily, only to hear Dan's all-too-familiar response: "I just wish I could move my legs. Maybe this is the day I'll be able to walk." And there he'd sit for the rest of the period, thinking about his legs, watching them for movement, rarely lifting an arm or pushing a weight.

This frustrated me to no end. *Are you blind!* I thought. *Don't you see what you have? Just look at all the blessings and opportunities that are yours simply because you can move your hands. You have access to a freedom that I pray for, and you are too wrapped up in your own self-pity to see it.*

One night I found myself in the room of my friend, Rich Hullinger. I had noticed that Rich constantly wore leather braces on his wrists and hands. Near the beginning of my hospital stay I had worn similar braces in order to stretch my tendons, but it seemed odd that he would still be wearing them. That night I asked Rich about them. He explained to me that the break in his neck was one pinhead higher than mine, and that because of that he was unable to move his wrist up and down, or even hold it straight against the power of gravity.

I returned to my room and prepared for bed. I didn't sleep much that night; over and over I thought of how blessed I was that I could make that simple movement. Suddenly, I found within my own persona everything I hated in Dan. During the past few days I had spent the bulk of my time concentrating on what I didn't have, when I could have been focusing on what I *did* have. Centering my efforts on wishing I had different circumstances, I had become totally oblivious of the many blessings in my life. This oblivion had caused my outlook on life to become tarnished. It affected the way I dealt with others, my zeal for life, and most important, the way I felt about myself. However, with this new realization of how much I did have, and how much I had taken for granted, I began to feel more blessed. As I felt more blessed, I became more thankful. And as I became more thankful, I developed a sense of worth, which brought a newfound ability to overcome.

Choices

Why Did I Jump?

KIETH MERRILL

When I was a young man I lived in a small community close to the mountains. I was a lifeguard and did lots of swimming. We used to go tubing down rivers and do all those crazy things that advisers worry about but guys get excited about. We went swimming at a place called East Canyon, a beautiful man-made reservoir. The dam is in a narrow neck of the canyon between sheer rock walls.

We couldn't water-ski because none of us had boats, but we would do what we called cliff diving. We would climb up those rocks and dive into the reservoir. We'd always wear tennis shoes because the rocks were so sharp. We used to have a wonderful time. I guess I didn't realize how really dangerous it was.

After we had been there several times and pretty well knew the rocks, cliffs, and the water depth, two or three of us hard-core East Canyon divers got into the inevitable teenage contest of raw courage. One guy climbed up to where we always dove from and yelled down: "Hey! I'll bet I dare dive higher than anybody here!"

"Ah, go on!"

So he climbed up to the top of the dam. The dam was about fifty feet off the water. Diving into the air he arched into the water, and like a bunch of sheep we crawled up the rocks, out onto the dam, and all of us dove off. I don't know if you've ever jumped fifty feet—it's a long way. I could only think that, after all, the water was seventy feet deep and couldn't hurt all that much.

Well, that didn't satisfy my friend, and so he said, "All right, I'll do one better!" He climbed sixty feet up the side of the cliff. And not wanting to be outdone, I climbed up by him. After all, everyone was looking at me. I had a great suntan, and I was sure everyone expected me to do what he was doing. He swallowed hard, buried his fear, and from trembling knees arched his back, and floated through sixty feet of air into the water.

I was grateful nobody was watching me as I prepared for my dive. When he had cleared and seemed to be all right, I took courage and made my dive. By now the other members of our diving contest had backed down, figuring it was a little too high. But not my friend. He climbed on up to about seventy feet and once more prepared to dive. From below I could barely see him. Seventy feet is a very long way up on the rocks. I said to myself, "I hope he doesn't do it because if *he* does it, then obviously *I've* got to do it, and I really don't want to." About then I saw a pink body float through the air and splash into the water not far from me. He came up laughing, rubbing his shoulders and his eyes, and said, "Well, Merrill, are you going to do it?"

"Of course, I'm going to do it!" Everybody on the shore said, "Yeah, of course he's going to do it!"

And so I swam back to the shore and climbed up the rocks. I knew I only had the courage for one more jump. I knew if I jumped at seventy feet, he was going to go higher, so I thought, "Well, I might as well go up to the very top where there is no way he can go higher."

I scrambled up eighty feet to the very top of the cliff. As I turned around and looked down, I saw that the cliffs were back away from the water at that height. I had two challenges: to fall eighty feet and to get enough clearance to avoid hitting the rocks at the bottom. Everybody was egging me on in a negative way. "You're chicken, you're chicken!"

I stood there all alone, everybody waiting down below. The water was so far away it looked like crinkled tinfoil in the sun. I was just terrified. I was committed, but I had not even based my decision on what I wanted to do or what I felt was right. I had based it on about a half dozen guys whose names I don't even remember who were yelling, "Hey, chicken, are you going to do it?"

I realized that in order to make the jump I would have to run a distance to get enough momentum to carry me over the rocks below. So I backed up and ran as hard as I could toward the edge. I found the mark I had carefully laid at the edge of the rock and sprang out into space. I don't know how long it takes to fall eighty feet, but for me it took about a week. On the way down I remembered distinctly how my parents and teachers had taught me to be careful when making decisions because I could kill myself with a wrong one. I said to myself, "You have done it; you have killed yourself, because when you hit the water you'll be going so fast that it might as well be concrete." And when I hit the water, I was sure it was concrete. I don't know how far down you go when you jump from eighty feet, but I was a grateful lad when my head finally popped above water. I took a quick inventory to make sure that the throbbing pain in my right thigh didn't designate the loss of anything important.

Well, why did I jump? Did I prove myself to the guys? You think they cared? You think they're sitting at home now saying, "Remember old Merrill, brave old Merrill, jumping off the . . ." They don't even remember! They don't care! But for me that moment was as important as my life. I made what could have easily been a *fatal* decision. Through the grace of a very patient Heavenly Father I wasn't killed. I didn't land on the rocks; I missed by only a few feet. I didn't drown, and I didn't have a concussion or a number of other things that could easily have happened because of such a stupid decision.

I was subjected to pressure that was hard to withstand, the pressure of friends expecting things of me that I didn't want to do because I knew better. But I yielded to the pressure. I was living in the world, and at that moment I was of the world because I was not in control of myself. I was not making decisions about my own life. The world made the decisions for me. Because I was of the world I barely avoided being in the world about six feet deep.

That's the way decisions are. They are either made by us, or they're made by the circle of people around us. And there are many voices talking to us when we make decisions. There are the voices of friends, parents, teachers, and others. We should listen to some of the voices. We should reject others, because not all voices give good counsel. As you face the challenge of being *in* but not *of* the world, recognize that *you* must make the decisions about your life. Be assured that if the world makes decisions for you, you will be of the world, and there's no way to avoid it.

Extra Squeezes of Cheese—and Other Lessons in Honesty

RICHARD G. MOORE

I am not cheap. At least, I don't consider myself to be cheap. Sure, there were those stories that went around the high school about me. One story recounts the time that I took a date to the junior prom. According to the legend, after the dance was over and we got into the car, I asked her if she was hungry and when she said, "Yes," I opened the glove compartment and pulled out two apples. At this point I would like to set the record straight. It was *not* the junior prom, I did it for a joke, and hey— she ate both apples!

I suppose I am a frugal person. While I was growing up, my family did not have a lot of money, and as an adult I have kept that tradition going. I consider myself to be a wise and careful shopper. I like to get my money's worth, and I do look for bargains. But surely frugality is a virtue. Is it wrong to want to pay less and get more? And are there people who would not want to get even more than what they paid for if they could? On the other hand, can this kind of thinking lead a person to rationalize their way onto the road of dishonesty?

As a teenager I worked for a time at a gas station and truck stop. It did not have a market or restaurant, but it did have the typical vending machines with candy and sodas. A trucker came in one day and bought a soda while his vehicle was being refueled. He put fifteen cents into the machine (I know, it was a long time ago), made his selection, and received a drink and a dime in change. It was long before my time that sodas cost only a nickel, so it was clear that something was wrong with the machine.

He tried the machine again. This time he put in a nickel and pushed the button. He got a drink and a dime in change. He did it again with the same results. "What are you drinking?" he hollered out the door to his partner. Pretty soon he was buying drinks for everybody. I was an employee and was standing right there, but it did not seem to bother him. As he walked out the door with an armful of sodas he said to me, "Darn fine machine you got here, kid."

I just stood there. I didn't report the situation to my boss, nor did I think, *What a dishonest person!* Instead, I remember thinking, *This is a darn fine machine!* as I put my own dime into the coin slot. I pushed the button. Nothing. I put in another nickel and pushed the button. Nothing. I put in another fifteen cents and pressed my selection. Nothing. I hit the side of the machine with my hand. Pain. Then I told my boss there was something wrong with the vending machine.

As I look back on that experience it is very clear to me that even though I did not benefit, I was still dishonest, because the intent and the attempt were both there. I have no excuse for my actions. I had been taught by my parents to be honest. Maybe because it was a machine I didn't think it was so bad. Or maybe I just saw an opportunity to get something for nothing with no one being the wiser. I have heard it said that the true measure of the integrity of people is what they would do if they knew they would not get caught.

After this experience I had to remind myself that I was basically an honest person. I was not a thief, nor did I cheat in school or lie to people. Now, if I could just watch myself on the little things, I would be completely honest. I had learned my lesson. Or had I?

The years went by, with me striving to be an honest person. After serving a mission and going to college I found myself living in Arizona. I had been married in the temple and was active in the Church. I considered myself to be an obedient, decent, and very honest person.

One Saturday after going to the temple in Mesa, my wife, Lani, and I stopped at a convenience store on the way back home. It was a hot day, so we bought a couple of sodas. (There is no pattern here. The sodas are only a coincidence.) My wife paid for the drinks and we got back on the road. About twenty minutes of driving later she said, "We have to go back!"

"What? Back where?"

"Back to the store where we bought the sodas. They gave me too much change," she explained.

"How much too much?" I asked.

"A dime."

"Oh, I'm not driving all the way back there for a dime," I announced. "It's only a dime; it doesn't matter . . . they won't even miss it."

"It's not how much it is that matters," she responded. "It is being honest that matters to me."

I didn't say anything. The thought crossed my mind that I had been to the temple that day and that in order to get there I had been asked by both my bishop and my stake president if I was honest.

Lani said, "You don't have to take me back now, but in a few weeks when we go to the temple again, can we stop by that store and return the dime?"

"Sure. No problem."

My wife was and is an honest person. I had thought of myself as an honest person, but maybe I was simply a person who did honest things *most* of the time. There is a difference. I had learned my lesson. Or had I?

Some years later we had moved from Arizona to Utah. Not far from our home was a convenience store (relax, there are no sodas in this story). At this little store there was a do-it-yourself nacho deal. A person would buy a little basket for the nachos and then put in as many or as few as he wanted for the same price. I loved the nachos, and I enjoyed loading my own because I am Captain Get-Your-Money's-Worth. Perhaps I went beyond what was prudent or in accordance with the spirit of the nacho law.

Instead of piling them in the basket, I racked them up like Pringles. Then I would line the edges of the basket with chips to give greater height to the basket and would pile chips on top of that to ease the embarrassment that the Pringle look might cause me when I got to the counter. One time the cashier said to me in an admiring way, "Boy, you really know how to load those chips up." I figured if it didn't bother him it shouldn't bother me.

What did bother me was the cheese machine. There was a big plunger that when pushed would dispense melted cheese. A sign on the cheese machine read: "ONLY TWO SQUEEZES OF CHEESE ALLOWED FOR EACH NACHO ORDER." Two squeezes did not provide enough cheese for a regular order of nachos, and it wasn't even close to enough for the army of chips I assembled. There was the rub. Nothing was said about the number of chips a person could take, but a cheese regulation had been put in force. I reasoned (I rationalized) that if I didn't push the plunger all the way in or let it all the way out, it did not constitute one complete squeeze. My application of cheese was a series of jerky motions, pushing in some, letting out a little, pushing in a little more, letting out a little, and pushing in until the plunger could be pushed no farther. Repeated twice.

It sounded like this:

One . . . n . . . n . . . n.

Twooooooo . . . oooooooooooo . . . ooooooooo . . . oooooo.

Two squeezes.

I got this type of order of nachos three or four times. The night after my most recent nacho expedition I had a temple recommend interview with the bishop. I answered each question honestly and felt good about my worthiness to go to the temple. Then the bishop asked if I was completely honest in all my dealings. As I was about to answer yes, an image of nachos came to my mind.

"Let me ask you a question, Bishop," I said.

He laughed when I told him about the extra squeezes of cheese, and he said he thought it was a good sign that my conscience was troubled by this kind of thing. "It shows that the Holy Ghost is at work," he said. "Many people might believe they are

142

honest but not worry about the so-called little things. Those who are truly honest or are striving to be truly honest will watch themselves on the little things as well as the big things."

He signed my recommend and told me to avoid those extra squeezes of cheese. All dishonesty, large or small, is still dishonesty. I had learned my lesson. Or had I?

A couple of years later I was in Salt Lake City looking for treasures in the basement of a used-book store. Carefully going over each title in the Church book section, I came across a book that didn't seem to fit. The title of the book was *The Flying Squadron*. I pulled the book from the shelf, wondering how it ended up in the Church book section. Inside the front cover of the book was a letter. The book had been a Christmas gift, and the letter was signed by the giver: Heber J. Grant. The discovery jolted me. President Grant's signature is not particularly rare, nor would collectors give much money for it, but that was not the point. This letter that I held in my hands had been signed by a prophet of God.

The price of the old book was ten dollars. I would readily pay ten dollars for the book with the letter in it, but did the owners of the store even know about the letter? The thought crossed my mind, *You wouldn't even have to buy the book. It's just a piece of paper in a book. You could put it in your pocket and no one would know. The bookstore people wouldn't be out anything, because they can still sell the book.*

I want to make it clear that these thoughts simply passed through my mind. In no way did I even consider taking the letter. This is called temptation. Temptation is not a sin. Giving in to temptation is a sin. I believe that seriously pondering temptation is a sin. There was no pondering this temptation. Close on the heels of these thoughts of dishonesty planted by the adversary came the incredulous voice of the Spirit: *The paper is valuable to you because it is signed by a prophet of God. Prophets of God are important to you because of the saving truths of the gospel they reveal. Now, the adversary would like you to steal the signature of a prophet of God!*

I shook my head and laughed at the ludicrousness of the temptation. Then I took the book to the counter and said, "I'd like to buy this book. Did you know that there was a letter in the book signed by Heber J. Grant?"

"Oh, of course," the man behind the counter replied. "That's why we can sell the book for ten dollars. Otherwise we couldn't give the book away."

I bought the book, and I have the letter with President Grant's signature. It reminds me that part of growing up spiritually is to become completely honest. And until the time that we arrive at a state of complete honesty, we are to constantly do honest things and resist temptations of dishonesty. We do until we become. After that, we do because we are.

$\mathcal{H}$ow We Live Today

JACK R. CHRISTIANSON

$\mathbf{M}$y brother was a car dealer when I reached the wonderful age when I could start driving. He purchased for me and my older sister a 1962 white Cadillac convertible with power everything. We called it the "White Stallion."

In May 1970 my friend Taylor Manning and I drove the White Stallion up Provo Canyon to Sundance Ski Resort. We wanted to drive up the canyon with the top down, just for fun. As three o'clock approached we headed back down the canyon so I would not be late for my job at Kentucky Fried Chicken. When we came out of the mouth of the canyon, we decided to take a different way home. That little decision would soon change forever the way I looked at life.

We barreled down North University Avenue at about seventy miles per hour (that was the speed limit in those days). The traffic coming the other way was thick, but we paid little attention to it as we effortlessly glided down the highway.

It wasn't long before we noticed a group of boys standing at the roadside. We found out later that they were a Little League baseball team on their way home from a practice. They stood waiting for a break in the traffic so they could cross the road.

I slowed down a little and watched them closely. There was a brief break in the traffic in the oncoming lane, so, without looking in our direction, two of the boys bolted into the street, right in front of us.

It all happened in an instant. I slammed my foot on the brakes and made some quick judgments. If I continued moving straight, I would hit the two ten-year-olds. If I veered to the right,

I would hit several of the boys. The only escape from tragedy was to the left, into the lane of oncoming traffic. The decision made, I steered to the left, but at the same time, the two boys heard the screaming of the tires on the pavement, and they looked up. One stopped and jumped back. The other jumped forward. The front end missed him, but the car plunged off the road into a weed-filled patch of field, tipped onto the passenger side door, and skidded through the field into a ditch. Miraculously, the car didn't roll and crush us. We had turned 180 degrees, coming to a full stop facing the direction from which we had come. The dust settled, and we realized the Cadillac was a total wreck. We were mad! "Let's go get them!" one of us said.

We jumped from the car to an unexpected horror. We thought we had missed both boys, but we hadn't. The boy who had jumped forward had been hit by our back bumper as we screeched past him. He had been caught in the thigh and knocked about 150 feet down the road.

When Taylor and I reached him it was an ugly scene. He had a compound fracture in one leg, his head was cut severely, and where he had skidded across the asphalt he had no skin.

I started to go into shock but didn't know it. At that moment I could think only that I should pray. So I did. I knelt right on the road and sought guidance.

People came from all around to help us. We were able to stop the boy's bleeding. Then we waited for the ambulance. As we worked with some valiant people to preserve this ten-year-old life, many of his friends, caught up in the emotion of the moment, yelled, "You killed Michael! You killed Michael! You crazy drunken driver. You killed Michael!" I'll never forget those screams as long as I live. They pierced me to the core.

What if I *had* been drinking? What if I had been using drugs? Thank goodness I hadn't, but what if I had?

The highway patrolman arrived and took over first aid for the boy. Then the ambulance came and rushed Michael to the hospital in Provo.

There were other ambulances as well. Another carload of

people required medical attention. Their car had been coming the other way and had driven off the highway to avoid a head-on collision with our car. The car was full of Cub Scouts. Many of them were hurt. It was a nightmare!

As Taylor and I walked to the patrol car with the officer, he said, "Boys, I sure hope we don't find any drugs or alcohol in the car or in your bloodstream. That boy may not survive."

I sobbed through my tears, "I live the Word of Wisdom! I live the Word of Wisdom!" He didn't have any idea what I was talking about.

As we walked I saw a baseball glove and a pair of baseball shoes lying in the road. I realized they were Michael's. A sick feeling swept over me. "I killed him!" I said to myself, and then began crying.

Taylor and I went through all the tests, which proved we had not been drinking or doing drugs. It was embarrassing, as people drove by slowly, gazing at two sixteen-year-olds with the officers.

I reflected for a moment. At eight o'clock that morning I couldn't have known that two ten-year-old boys would dart in front of my car in the afternoon. What if I had been just "eating, drinking, and being merry"? What if we had just had one drink for the road, or just tried it once, and that once was that day in May?

No one knows what the future holds, so we had better not just "eat, drink, and be merry," because tomorrow we may die!

We finally made it to the hospital emergency room to see if Michael was going to recover. As we walked in we saw a tall, distinguished-looking man with his arms around a crying woman. The highway patrol officer introduced me to the couple. They were Michael's parents. I fell into the big man's arms and cried for him to forgive me. He told me that the accident had been explained to him. He understood it wasn't my fault and that I had done the only thing that could have been done. He assured me there would be no lawsuit.

Then he shocked me. "Young man," he said. "I don't know if you are a Latter-day Saint or not. But I am. I have been into the operating room and given my son a priesthood blessing. I believe he'll be just fine and I don't want you to worry."

At the time I didn't understand the full meaning of what he was saying. But in the many years since, I have pondered it often. He was worthy at that moment to use his priesthood to save the life of his son. He didn't have to run home to repent. At the start of his day he couldn't have known that he would need to give his son a lifesaving blessing that day. What if he had been viewing pornography the night before? What if he had decided that one alcoholic drink or one cup of coffee was okay? What if he had been eating, drinking, and merrymaking? Would he have felt worthy to perform that critical administration?

We simply don't know what the future holds. We don't know when our time in mortality is up and when we will be brought before our Maker. We easily forget how fragile, brief, and precious life really is. We seem to need reminding.

How we live today does make a difference. We can repent and improve today. We can keep moving forward—not eating, drinking, and being merry; but living, loving, and learning.

"To Every Thing There Is a Season"

CARLOS E. ASAY

Sally was a beautiful, precocious girl who wanted to grow up too fast. At the ripe old age of fifteen she prevailed upon her parents to allow her to date. Her parents really did not like the idea, but Sally wearied them with her pleadings and they reluctantly gave their consent.

The first few dates included other young couples. Soon, however, group dating ceased and Sally and her partner went to shows, dances, and other places by themselves. More and more time was spent in secluded settings, and step by step the physical contacts increased. What started out as harmless hand-holding grew steadily into something very intimate and very serious.

Early in her sixteenth year, Sally became pregnant. Though her boyfriend was not much older than she and still attending high school, it was decided that they would be married. A wedding ceremony was held in the privacy of the home in which Sally had been reared, and the two immature youths began their marriage.

Both Sally and her husband became school dropouts, for she was with child and he had to scramble for a job. Even before the baby was born the couple began to argue over their forced circumstances. Both yearned for the companionships of friends in school; both missed the church and school activities being enjoyed by peers; both resented the restrictions and responsibilities of married life; and both felt uneasy about their dependency upon Sally's parents for a place to live, the payment of medical bills, and other necessities. Each began to blame the other for all that had happened causing them to enter the adult arena before either was prepared.

When the baby came, things settled down for a few weeks. The young couple loved their daughter and delighted in being parents, although they had to rely upon others for the care of the child. But in due time the novelty of having a baby wore out and the heavy responsibilities of a family became a reality, especially to Sally's husband. He worried about supporting a wife and child—he wasn't certain that he could do it. And he wondered whether this new role as husband and father was really one he wanted to assume.

Soon after her seventeenth birthday the inevitable happened. Sally's husband asked for a divorce, saying that he really didn't love her and that married life was not for him—at least not for now.

So at the ripe old age of seventeen, Sally's life came apart. Here she was a mother, a divorcée, a school dropout, a burden to her parents, and still not even old enough to vote. She had few skills and no training; yet she was faced with the prospects of finding a way to support herself and daughter. She longed for the more carefree days of yesterday while overwhelmed by the responsibilities of today and tomorrow. Deep down within her heart she wished she had been more discreet in her relationship with the opposite sex and more patient in growing up. She wished she had been less hard of heart and more susceptible to the counsel given by loved ones.

Sally's sad experience helps to verify the wisdom found in the words of the Preacher, who said: "To every thing there is a season, and a time to every purpose under the heaven" (Ecclesiastes 3:1). Yes, there is a time to be born, a time to be a child, a time to be a youth, a time to be an adult, and even a time to die. Each season and time has its purpose and each is a part of the eternal rhythm of life.

Those who believe that God has "made every thing beautiful in his time" (Ecclesiastes 3:11) will respect the eternal rhythm and take matters in proper sequence, knowing that if they do so they can claim all the blessings life can give.

Sticks and Stones

JOHN BYTHEWAY

Sticks and stones can break my bones, but names can never
   hurt me.
But oh, the hurt I feel inside when friends I've known desert me!
For now I'm left to walk the crowded halls of school alone,
And wonder what's been said today, when the whispering is
   done.
And when I kneel to pray at night, I shed a little tear
And ask for Heavenly Father's love, and trust He will be near.
Now, if you want to break some bones, some sticks and stones
   will do,
But if you want to break a heart, just spread a lie or two.
'Cause sticks and stones may break some bones, but broken
   bones can mend,
But spread around an evil fib, and the hurt may never end.

Prom Dress

ELAINE CANNON

Our family-owned shop, "The Dressmaker," in Foothill Village, was a hub for girls and their mothers to come to for fabric and design ideas for proms, weddings, Sunday-best dresses. One day I was measuring yardage for two girls who attended a private Catholic school nearby. Over at the pattern corner a mother and her daughter, Stacey, sat arguing over formal patterns. Stacey was nearly out of control. Her mother wouldn't agree to a strapless formal design. The young woman raised her voice, using words like *stupid, archaic, kindergarten frocks.* The mother held her ground, talking about Church standards, and the teenage girl groaned loudly, "Oh, Mother!" It was clear that the young woman was not only living in the world but partaking of it heavily.

The two other customers and I couldn't help but hear the argument and witness the tantrum. The shop was not large. But when Stacey came crying over to the counter, the two girls from the Catholic boarding school took things out of my hand. "I couldn't help overhearing your fight with your mom," one of them said to Stacey. "Come on. What difference does the style make? Get a new dress, go to your dance, and smile a lot." She was practical.

Then the other one spoke. "Look. You are a Mormon girl. I am a Catholic one. You think you have the only restrictions? Forget it. It's called growing up safe. At our school we can't even wear anything sleeveless, let alone strapless. Even if we defy the rules, it doesn't get us anywhere; the sisters have a box by the door at the dance—a box full of jackets and scarves to shroud us

153

with if our formals aren't modest enough. Hey, we've survived. We're seniors. We're happy. Come on, kid, don't hassle your mom. I just wish I could be home with mine to hear her approval when I leave for the dance."

Stacey didn't say thanks to the girls, but she did quit crying and bought the pattern her mother had approved.

I've thought a lot about that incident. Sometimes the "not just ordinary" youth haven't been baptized—yet. Sometimes Church membership doesn't insure stalwart youth; it should, but there is that matter of agency—one must *choose* to listen, to learn, to obey.

$\mathscr{D}$ress and Appearance

RANDALL C. BIRD

Some time ago, while presenting a fireside to a group of youth, I invited two young people to come to the stand and respond to a question. To the young man I said: "I would like you to visit a high school in this community and bring back to this group any young woman that you perceive to be 'wild.' By *wild*, I mean one who has questionable morals, language, and feelings of self-worth. Do you think you could pick out and bring back such a person by just observing her appearance and conduct?" The same question was asked of the young woman, only I asked her to return with a young man of the same characteristics.

It was interesting to note that both of these young people said they could easily do such a thing. I then asked them to describe the appearance of the person they would bring back. The young man mentioned things like too much makeup, tight-fitting pants, wild hair, an abundance of jewelry, and so forth. The young woman said that the boy she returned with would also wear tight-fitting jeans, maybe even with holes in them. Heavy metal T-shirts, excessive jewelry, and foul language were some other traits that her returning young man would possess.

It should be noted that both of these imaginary people were labeled virtually by their appearance alone. Aside from the matter of speech they could be fine individuals, but by the way they appeared they were judged to be wild.

Daily our dress, grooming, and general appearance are being evaluated by those around us. We need to dress, speak, and act so that we reflect an image which enhances womanhood, magnifies manhood, and exemplifies sainthood.

The Happy Slow Thinker

EDGAR A. GUEST

Full many a time a thought has come
   That had a bitter meaning in it.
And in the conversation's hum
   I lost it ere I could begin it.

I've had it on my tongue to spring
   Some poisoned quip that I thought clever;
Then something happened and the sting
   Unuttered went, and died forever.

A lot of bitter thoughts I've had
   To silence fellows and to flay 'em,
But next day always I've been glad
   I wasn't quick enough to say 'em.

Testimony
and
Missionary Work

A Relationship with God

A. DAVID THOMAS

I remember a young man who desired to have a real relationship with God. His own father had died and he needed a paternal influence in his life. He was sixteen, almost seventeen, and as big as a man, but that didn't mean he wasn't lonely or afraid. You can be that size, have lots of friends and a mother who loves you, and still be lonely and afraid. He had heard all of his life about how God loved him, about how God understood, cared, and could help. He desired such a relationship.

He had been taught about being good. He had been baptized. He prayed every day, but he didn't feel he had the relationship he was looking for. So he sought to refine his life in an effort to make himself right with God so that they could talk. He was careful about his speech and the stories he listened to. He was even careful about whom he hung around with. Certain movies and music didn't seem quite right anymore. He started reading the scriptures again. His prayers changed. They weren't a religious duty anymore or an exercise he did so that he could go to sleep without feeling uncomfortable. He really tried to talk to God. He felt he was making some real progress and decided to put a whole day, an extra day, aside for Heavenly Father. On this day he would be very careful not to crowd God out. He even decided to fast—not eat or drink for a whole day. He did it, but at the conclusion of his fast his answer, the response, had not come. He wanted to know whether God loved him, and he hadn't received an answer.

Teenagers can be such believers. This young man knew the trouble wasn't God—it must be him. Not enough time. Not enough faith. Not enough real intent in his desire. He decided to wait and, not thinking, he went to bed hungry.

The next day was Saturday—a special day for a teenager. He looked out of the window, and to his delight it had snowed. My friend was a skier and had a season pass to a local ski resort. Now he had no thought of breakfast or of his quest for his relationship with God—just six inches of new powder and a glorious, sun-filled day. He enjoyed a morning of skiing—excellent skiing.

Then it happened. In the tram on his way up for another run, he felt strange. He was sixteen and "cool," so he couldn't let on that he wasn't feeling right. Standing up, he locked his knees and leaned against the wall of the tram. The next thing he knew he was lying face down on the floor of the tram. He had fainted from lack of food. He crawled on all fours and sat up with his back against the wall. He realized he would have to make up his mind about what he wanted most. He could continue his day of perfect skiing—a glorious day, fresh powder (how many days like this would he have to ski?). The other option: his quest for closeness with his Heavenly Father. He felt he could only pursue one option—eat and ski, or continue in his quest to find God. And he knew he wanted God more than he wanted a good day of skiing.

As he rode the tram back down the mountain, he felt a rage building up in his heart. In his mind he yelled at God: What does it take? What do you want from me? At the bottom he opened the trunk of his car and took out a pair of shoes, since he couldn't drive with his ski boots on. He strapped his skis into the carrier on the roof of the car. He opened the car door and slid behind the wheel and started the engine. Then the rage hit again. "God, what do you want?" he yelled. "How much does it take to get you to speak to me?" In frustration, he slugged the dashboard helplessly. But as quickly as the rage arrived, it departed. He felt ashamed, and worried that somehow he had spoiled something or had failed an important test. He didn't know that God will often take you to the edge—to the extreme—to stretch you. But he never departs. He knows where the breaking point is. My young friend had not failed—far from it!

He bowed his head and pleaded with God not to give up on him. He asked the Lord to overlook his outburst, and he started to drive away. By force of habit he slipped a cassette into his car stereo as he pulled out of the parking lot. A quiet peacefulness settled over his soul. It was as if the outlet of his rage and the repentance that followed it had cleansed him, and nothing stood in his way. The road was clear, the mountains were dazzling with their new, pearl-white vestments. Below him the bowl of the valley was resplendent—a rainbow of color dancing in the clarity of a beautiful afternoon. He was overcome by the purity of it all. He pulled the car to the side of the road so that he could just look at it.

And then it happened. A gentle, warm flow of assurance moved over him. It started in his legs and moved up through his body, through his arms and his neck and head; a wonderful sense of "all is well," peace and control. It was then that his mind focused on the music and on the words of the cassette he had casually slipped into the stereo:

> All you've got to do is call,
> And I'll be there—
> You've got a friend.

The words of Carole King filled his heart and mind, and it seemed as if someone spoke to him. A voice inside him said: "My friend, that's how I feel about you. You can count on me. I love you. You are my son. *You can count on me!*" The sweet, gentle assurance remained with him. He turned off the stereo, looked at the magnificent view for a few more moments, and then pulled back onto the highway. He had received his answer. God knew where he was. He was loved. He had a relationship he could count on.

They Knew

ELAINE CANNON

While I was the Church's general president of the Young Women I visited Taiwan. In Taipei the youth chorus behind the podium provided inspiring music for the visit of general Church officers from Salt Lake City, Utah. I was overcome with joy as I studied row after row of attractive, fresh-looking, black-haired young men and young women. They were the chosen generation of Taiwan. They listened intently to every speaker and sang their hearts out on cue.

When it was time for us to leave, the President of The Church of Jesus Christ of Latter-day Saints turned toward this practiced chorus and waved his white handkerchief so they could pick him out of the pressing crowd. It was stunning to see an all-inclusive change come over that group. It was as if a signal had been given, as if a water tap had been turned on. Tears streamed down the cheeks of every boy and girl as they waved back. What joy! They knew they were in the presence of a prophet of God. They *knew* that this man was the mouthpiece of God on earth at this time. All of us knew that they knew, and we began weeping as well.

$\mathcal{H}$ow I Know: A Convert's Shoes

CHRIS CROWE

In the final semester of my senior year in high school, Ms. Keller, an enthusiastic, bright, and liberal student teacher, replaced stodgy old Mr. Potter as our American Government teacher. She was full of new ideas, one of which she explained on her first day of class. "People are more important than books and tests." She interrupted our applause to add, "That doesn't mean we won't use books and have tests, but it does mean that I want everyone to get to know each other as individual human beings right from the beginning."

For our first assignment we had to present ourselves to the class in a creative way. "Open yourselves up to us," she said, sitting atop Mr. Potter's desk. "Let us know what's really important to you and your life."

Great! I thought. One of the important people in my life had just dumped me—said she couldn't date me anymore—and *she* was the last thing I wanted to talk about right then.

Still, the project appealed to me, not because I liked touchy-feely pop psychology stuff but because I liked assignments that could be completed without cracking a book, writing a paper, or darkening the door of the library. And this would give me something to do to take my mind off my former girlfriend. She was a Mormon, I wasn't, and for reasons I still didn't understand she let her religion come between us and end what I thought was a beautiful relationship.

Anyway, after racking my brains for several days I finally decided on a presentation I was sure would impress Ms. Keller.

On the day our presentations were due I showed up to class

wearing a shirt and tie and carrying a large paper grocery sack. In it was one shoe of every kind that I owned. When it was my turn I set my unpaired shoes on the table in front of the class and, ignoring the odor jokes from my buddies in the front row, began to explain how my various shoes represented not only me but also what was important to me.

Lined up across the table like a row of used cars was one of my football shoes, a basketball shoe, a track shoe, a running shoe, a shoe I played racquetball in, a house slipper, a shoe I wore to school and when I hung out with friends, and, last of all, a shiny but slightly dusty wingtip, a shoe that I wore to church—when I went. I talked, more seriously than I ever had in class before, about sports, my home and family, friends, school, and church and explained why they were important parts of my life.

When my allotted time was up I sat down, relieved to be fin-ished—such serious and personal talk always made me uncom-fortable—and satisfied that my presentation had gone well.

The next student, Jimmy, walked up to the front of the room and set two books on the table, a long rectangular one and a paperback. "This is my book of remembrance," he said, holding up the long one. "It's a record of me and the important events in my life." He flipped it open and showed us photos, charts, and certificates, stopping every once in a while to explain one and why it was significant.

Finally he set it down and picked up the paperback. "This is the Book of Mormon," he said. "The way I live my life, the things I believe, and the things I hope for—they're all based on this book."

Oh no, I thought as I slid down in my chair, *a goody-goody Mormon. These guys are so corny.*

Jimmy spoke for a few more minutes, finally ending with a catch in his voice, ". . . and I know it's true. I *know* it's true . . . ," —he paused for a moment to gulp down his emotion—". . . and I'm glad I know. I say these things in the name of Jesus Christ, amen." A couple other voices in the room quietly echoed "amen." As I watched him walk back to his desk I noticed that a few stu-dents around me were teary eyed.

I didn't know for sure, but I guessed they were Mormons too. The few times my old girlfriend had dragged me to her church I had noticed that Mormons liked to say they *knew* this and *knew* that and that they often got teary eyed when they talked about their religion. Normally I would have shrugged off a presentation like Jimmy's as cornball religious stuff, but that day, for some reason, it didn't seem so corny. Instead, it made me curious. Why could they say they *knew* their church was true when at best all I could say about mine was that I believed in it?

I watched them after class talking quietly together on their way out the door, patting each other on the back. *How can they know?* I wondered. *How can they?*

A month or two later I was up in my bedroom, alone, not particularly troubled or unhappy, but thoughtful. In the top drawer of my desk lay a paperback copy of *A Marvelous Work and a Wonder,* a parting gift from my old Mormon girlfriend.

Thinking of her and recalling Jimmy's presentation and other conversations I'd had with Mormon kids, I pulled the book out and began reading. Maybe it would help me understand why it was they could talk about *knowing* their church was true.

The opening pages contained Joseph Smith's story of his first vision, and as I read it, it struck me that this man, or boy, or whoever he was, was telling the truth. It was quite simple and plain and logical to me—no blaring trumpets or burning bosoms but straightforward bright lights emanating from the heavenly messengers. I set the book down on my desk and felt a surge of quiet confidence—a feeling I now recognize as the Holy Ghost—confirm what I had just read.

Such sudden and sure knowledge startled me because I realized that if Joseph Smith's story was true, the church he founded under heavenly direction must also be true. As I pondered my newly discovered testimony, I knew that I'd have to do something about it, though I wasn't sure what. I decided that tomorrow I'd give my old Mormon girlfriend a call and tell her I *knew* what she and her friends knew and ask her if she had any ideas about what I should do next.

Well, she had plenty of ideas, and the busy weeks of missionary discussions, fasting, and prayer that followed only served to confirm what I had first realized after reading Joseph Smith's story one spring afternoon in my bedroom: It's true. I know it!

$\mathcal{He}$ Wanted a Testimony

R. SCOTT SIMMONS

My wife and I had occasion to be up in Canada, where we happened to be staying over a weekend, and so we decided to slip into a ward up there and attend sacrament meeting. It turned out to be a missionary farewell. I love missionary farewells, so I was really excited about this.

The missionary's brothers and sisters spoke, the mom and dad spoke, and then the missionary spoke. And I'll never forget this young man. He stood up and said, "I think a lot of you are probably surprised to see me here," and as soon as he said it, every head started to shake yes. Now, my wife and I didn't know who this young man was—we had just snuck into this ward, so we didn't know any of the background—but evidently it had taken some doing to get him on his mission. He continued, "And most of you probably think that I might not have a testimony, but I want you to know that I do, and I want to tell you how I got that testimony."

He said that he went to his mom and said, "Mom, I don't think I have a testimony." And his mom said, "Do you want one?" He said, "Yeah, yeah, I do." And she said, "Then I will tell you how to get a testimony." She looked at her son and she said, "I promise you that if you will read the Book of Mormon every day for a week, and then at the end of the week if you'll kneel down and apply Moroni's promise and ask Heavenly Father if it's true, you'll know that it is, and you'll have a testimony."

So that is what this young man did. He read every day for a week, and at the end of the week he knelt down and prayed, and nothing happened. He went to his mom and said, "Look, I did what you said and nothing happened." Now, under these circumstances it would be really easy for a parent just to say something like, "Well, thanks for tryin'," and let it go, but this good mother stuck to it. She said, "Tell me about your scripture reading." He said, "What do you mean?" She said, "When did you read your scriptures?" He said, "Well, I read them before I went to bed." She said, "How long did you read?" "Till I feel asleep"—which probably means, as it might for many of us, that he sometimes got as far as "And it came to pass" and then *boom*, good night!

She said—and I will never forget this—"How would you feel if Heavenly Father gave you the last few minutes of his day? What if Heavenly Father went about all his work and then for the last five minutes gave you attention?" Then this wonderful mother said, "I'll tell you what, let's schedule a time, a time that we can read every day, and I'll read with you." They decided that after school would be the best time, and so they picked that as their time. Neither one of them was a morning person, and so they thought that after school would be good and then it wouldn't be too late at night. And they read every day for a week.

Now at his missionary farewell this young man could hardly speak as he told about his experience of kneeling down and applying Moroni's promise. And then he said very simply, "Brothers and sisters, I know it's true. I know it's true."

The only thing he did different was he scheduled a time. He made scripture reading a priority in his life. Instead of just "working in" the Lord wherever he could, he put Him first.

Football and the Book of Mormon

JACK R. CHRISTIANSON

The Book of Mormon, a glorious treasure, has changed my life forever. I read it in seminary in the ninth grade. However, I did so only to fulfill my assignment and didn't give it much thought. At age eighteen, I left home to enter the world of college football. At the time I hadn't decided whether I would serve a mission. I wanted to play football. I thought of little else.

One night after a home game, I went with some of my teammates to an activity in a nearby city. We arrived home about 8:30 A.M. the following morning. It was Sunday, and priesthood meeting started at 9:00 A.M. I showered and walked to church at the institute of religion across the street from our dormitory. As I walked in, the bishop greeted me. He asked me a few questions, and then we went to his office to talk. I don't remember all we talked about, but I remember going back to the dorm determined to read the Book of Mormon, pray, and find out if it was true!

When I arrived back at the dorm, I pulled my scriptures from the shelf. The scriptures were a high school graduation gift from my parents. The previous year in seminary I had not missed a day of reading the Doctrine and Covenants, but I had not read for the entire summer.

I opened the Book of Mormon and began reading. Before long some of my teammates walked in and began giving me a difficult time. After that, I decided to read in private. Every morning I got up early and read and prayed. To this day I can remember finishing Moroni 10 and applying the magnificent promise found in verses 4 and 5.

That day I discovered that the book is true and I needed to

share it with others. Doing so, however, was not easy. I was on scholarship and was committed to play football. I felt my decision had been made. I would stay and play football and be a missionary by my actions.

Thanksgiving vacation came, and I returned home. After talking with my family, I went to visit my good friend Taylor Manning. Again, I thought my decision was made; that is, until I walked into Taylor's kitchen and saw him with a missionary haircut sitting at the table eating a bowl of cereal. "What happened to you?" I asked.

He responded, "I'm going on a mission, Ed!" (He always called me Ed for some reason.) He told me that he knew the Book of Mormon to be true and he wanted to serve his Father in Heaven. I knew it was true too . . . but, give up a football scholarship? I was stunned. However, it didn't take long before my testimony of the book, and Taylor's testimony, won the battle. When I went back to school, I talked with my coach and we worked out arrangements for when I would get back in two years. I went to the New Mexico and Arizona mission. Taylor went to the Netherlands. Neither of us would be where we are today had we not read and prayed about the Book of Mormon.

After coming home, I was able to play football for three more seasons. However, these last three seasons were focused on far more than just how far or how accurately I could throw a football. I had found out, to some extent, why I needed Christ.

Even at McDonald's

ARDETH G. KAPP

It was in Seattle, at McDonald's, under the big arches, on a Saturday night around 9:30 P.M. Two young men and four young women were huddled over a table in the corner with a good supply of napkins covering a major portion of the entire table. What were they doing?

The following morning was fast and testimony meeting. Near the close of the meeting, a young man walked to the podium. I was a visitor in the ward and did not ask his name, but I shall never forget his message or the spirit in which he shared his feelings. He began with a broad grin and then glanced from the corner of his eye at his friend who had been sitting by him in the audience.

"Well," he said, leaning on one side of the pulpit and then the other, "my friend and I received a call last night around 9:15. It was one of the girls from school." He hesitated and then explained, "She said she and three of her girlfriends from school were at McDonald's and were talking about us and what we believed and how we are different. She said they wanted us to come to McDonald's and tell them how come we are different."

The young man's smile enlarged; he may have been thinking that the girls' request was a new approach to get a couple of young guys to meet them on a Saturday night. He continued, "We weren't doing anything anyway, so we thought, why not?" He paused a moment, and his countenance changed. "They were serious," he said. "They really did want to know what we believed and what makes us different."

He told how, in an effort to answer their many questions, he

171

and his friend pulled a table to a corner of the restaurant, covered it with napkins, borrowed a pencil from one of the employees, and began their explanation. "On those napkins," he said, "we told the whole story. I drew three large circles representing the three degrees of glory, and we went from there. We told them about baptism, and they had lots of questions."

We all listened intently as this young man testified before the congregation of the truths he and his friend taught that night at McDonald's. "We were really pumped," he said. It was as though in answering the questions he discovered the strength of his own sure testimony. Indeed, these two young men were different. Through the baptismal covenant, they had committed to "stand as witnesses of God at all times and in all things, and in all places" (Mosiah 18:9). Yes, even at McDonald's. That night at McDonald's, two young men experienced the excitement and thrill of sharing something very precious with four young women who must have respected and trusted them and were now their friends, real friends.

$\mathscr{D}$on't You Have Anything Better to Do?

ALLAN K. BURGESS AND MAX H. MOLGARD

Igh school had been a fun time for Richard, and it was hard for him to see it come to an end. But he was also very excited about what lay ahead. Richard had received a scholarship to the very school he wanted to attend and had been accepted into the program of his dreams. As he attended school and got involved in his studies and in the various activities on campus, all of the facets of his life seemed to fit beautifully together. His first two years of college were everything he had dreamed of. Life was wonderful.

As summer approached, one of Richard's favorite professors asked him if he would be interested in a summer job that was related to Richard's major field of study. The more he talked with the professor, the more excited Richard got. Not only was this a great job but a great chance to meet some of the people whom he considered to be the best in his chosen profession. He told the professor that he wanted the job.

Richard started his summer job with enthusiasm. That excitement didn't let up all summer. He loved his job. For that matter, he loved his life—except for a nagging feeling in the back of his mind that he couldn't shake, no matter how hard he tried.

That nagging feeling had been with him ever since he had made the decision, once and for all, that he was not going to serve a mission. He had been raised in a family that had always talked about "the day you go on your mission," but his family had seemed to accept the fact that he wasn't going to serve. What was the problem? For some reason he could not get rid of the thought that a piece of his life was missing.

It didn't really make sense. Here he was, doing everything that he had ever dreamed about, yet he wasn't satisfied. As the summer drew to a close and the nagging feeling persisted, Richard made the decision to serve a mission. He was twenty-one years old, and he was going on a mission!

Several months passed. Richard had received his call and was making the final preparations to leave. The peace that he had been searching for had finally come. He knew he was doing the right thing and could hardly wait to expand his gospel knowledge and share it with others.

One week before entering the MTC, Richard went to the store to buy his two-year supply of white shirts. As he picked up his shirts, he saw a buddy from high school. Eyeing the neat white stack, his friend chuckled, "You must have settled down more than I thought you ever would. But your wardrobe is going to be kind of boring, isn't it?"

Richard smiled back and said, "My wardrobe might be kind of boring, but my life isn't going to be. I'm going to Spain on a mission."

"Spain? On a mission? You're kidding!" his friend sputtered. "Don't you have anything better to do?"

"No, I don't have anything better to do," was Richard's quick reply. And he grinned both inside and out because he knew that he really didn't have anything better to do.

"What Makes You the Way You Are?"

ELAINE CANNON

We were in a staff meeting for Church publications. The soldier was just back from military duty. He had joined the army right out of high school and left his little Mormon community as a real innocent, a high-principled person determined to keep God's commandments, no matter what!

He arrived at army camp, only to be assigned the bunk next to an older soldier who knew all the dirty words to say and said them, who knew all the wild things to do and did them. He kicked the youth kneeling in prayer at night. When alcoholic beverage was refused he forcefully pried open the Mormon's mouth to pour the liquor down his gullet. He spread pornographic pictures in the newcomer's bed so that when the young man turned back the bedding he couldn't avoid looking at them.

It was a miserable education for the farm boy with high ideals.

Then the troops went for overnight training on a cold plateau. The Mormon soldier had come prepared with two blankets. The hardened soldier had none. Temperatures dropped way down after midnight. The tough man lay there next to the kid and thought, *If this goody-goody were all that he pretends to be, he'd give me one of his blankets—I don't deserve it, but I need it.*

And as the thought crossed his mind, the hand of the young boy handed over a blanket. And that did it. The next morning the older soldier awakened his companion early and said, "All right. Tell me what makes you this way. How could you give me your blanket after all the stuff you've taken from me? You should have put a knife in my back and twisted it after all I've put you through. What is it that makes you the way you are?"

And so the young man told him.

The life-changing gospel was taught. The hardened soldier became a member of the Church, and his personal growth began. He wrote to his brother stationed with the army somewhere else and told him to "find the Mormons because they are for real." The brother did that and was baptized. The two of them then sent many letters to their sister in mid-USA and told her about the Church. She joined. When the former tough soldier returned home he was a different person and soon became a leader of youth in his stake.

All because one Mormon boy believed in God, had the courage to live his religion, and dared to share it.

She Wanted to Follow Heavenly Father's Plan

BARBARA BARRINGTON JONES

The first I knew of Gretchen Polhemus was when her father called me and asked if I, as someone who helps train young women for beauty pageants, would help his daughter. I usually only work with the state beauty pageant winners. I told him, "Well, she's not a state winner."

He said, "But you don't know my daughter. She's special."

Gretchen came to my house with beauty queens from Nevada and California. I didn't realize how much of a country girl she was.

I had the girls together for some training. I started at one end and said, "Now tell me, each one of you, what do you use on your hair?"

Gretchen said, "I go down to the feed store and I get something called Mane and Tail. I put that stuff on my hair, and it makes it so nice."

I tried to hide my surprise. "Oh, Mane and Tail, that sounds like a lovely beauty product."

The rest of the girls used normal things.

Then I asked, "Now, girls, what do you use on your fingernails?"

I started with Gretchen. She said, "I go down to the feed store and get a product called Hoof Alive. I rub that stuff on my fingernails, and it makes them hard, like horses' hooves."

All I could say was, "Oh, that's nice."

Then we talked about their pageant hairstyles. Gretchen said,

"Oh, you're talking about that hairstyle that looked like I had a cow patty plopped right on top of my head."

I was thinking, *This girl really is from Texas.*

We finished our training, and the girls were going to go down to Fisherman's Wharf, a fun tourist spot in San Francisco. Gretchen asked if she could stay with me.

I said, "Well, I'm doing a missionary zone conference, and you don't know what that is. You probably wouldn't like to go."

She just said that she would like to go with my husband and me.

We were a little late—you know Mormon Standard Time. Here were thirty-eight missionaries from the Santa Rosa Mission, and the zone conference had already started. I rushed up to the front and gave my talk. I finished, and then the missionaries started bearing their testimonies. As we were listening, Gretchen leaned over and whispered to me, "Can I go up there?"

I was amazed. "You want to go up there?"

She nodded.

I said, "Yes, it's okay."

She walked up to the front of the room. She had on a beautiful white dress with flowers all over it; she was in high heels with her hair up. Those missionaries had their mouths hanging open. She stood up in front of them and said: "I look out at all of you and am so proud of you. I never knew that this church existed until today. I'm just so proud of you that you're giving two years of your life to serve the Savior. You have been such an inspiration to me. I promise to be like you and dedicate my time to serving the Savior."

Now I want to let Gretchen tell you her own story:

"Do you believe that God has a plan for you? I do.

"The night I first competed for Miss Texas, I stood up there on the stage and the audience was in complete darkness. I had prepared and prayed to win, but I ended up second runner-up. I thought God had betrayed me. What went wrong? I wanted it for myself. I never bothered to ask if it was Heavenly Father's plan for me.

"The next year I told Heavenly Father that if he could use me more as Miss Texas than as just Gretchen, then I'd be Miss Texas. But if that was not in his plan, it would be fine. That night I walked out on stage, and I could see every face. I won and went on to win Miss USA. But I never had the feeling that 'I did it.' I wanted to follow Heavenly Father's plan for me, and this was part of it.

"I wondered how I was going to serve him for a whole year. He started to show me. Sometimes it isn't what you say that counts, it's how you act towards others. It's smiles. It's hugs. It's compliments. It's everything Christlike.

"I finished my year as Miss USA, and I started working for ESPN. And Barbara invited me to go with her on speaking assignments. Every time I would go with her into these church houses and to youth conferences I would feel something. I didn't know what it was, but it would make me cry. I had told the Lord that I would serve him, so I started speaking for a lot of other churches, but I never felt the same feeling there as I did in the LDS church.

"Barbara invited me to go to Japan to a big youth conference being held there, but she got sick and couldn't go. It's a fourteen-hour plane trip, and Brad Wilcox, another of the youth speakers, started telling me all about the Church. The neat thing was that nothing he said was scary to me. I was soaking it in all the way to Japan.

"At the end of the youth conference, before the testimony meeting, everyone sang, 'I Am a Child of God.' All these big tough football-player-type guys with long hair and black T-shirts, they all sang. That really hit me. The Spirit was touching my heart. I saw something in those kids that I didn't have. I'd done a lot in my life, but I wanted to be like them. I sat back and cried. I knew then and there that someday I would be a Mormon. I just didn't know when. I thought, 'Heavenly Father, this is so special, so important, that it's taken me three years to know about this church. But if I join now, it will be just on emotion. I want to make sure that you tell me, and it's not me telling you when.' Brad encouraged me to keep praying.

"Back in the United States, I was going to meet Barbara in Provo, Utah, for a conference at BYU. As we were coming over the mountains into Utah Valley we dropped lower preparing for the long approach to the Salt Lake airport. I was looking out of the window. It was a beautiful sight, with the sun setting and the lights shining on the temple in Provo. I leaned against the window and said: 'Heavenly Father, I'm waiting on you. I know you want me to join, but I don't know when. I'm waiting on you.'

"I heard a deep voice say, 'Yes.' I turned around to see if someone was sitting behind me. There was a woman, and I knew she hadn't said anything. I thought, 'Was that me or was that Heavenly Father?' Then this sweet voice said, 'Come follow me. It's time.'

"I couldn't wait to tell Barbara."

When Gretchen got off the plane, she was so excited. She said, "Barbara, guess what!"

I said, "You're going to be baptized."

She said, "How did you know?"

I had known that if she would be open the Lord would literally guide her to the Church, the place where she can serve him the best.

Gretchen's message for the youth is this: "I wish young people knew that if they would live like they are supposed to, staying close to the Savior, they can have anything they want, provided it's Heavenly Father's will. I learned that Heavenly Father does want us to work for things. If they are righteous desires and we present them to him and say, 'This is what I want; now, is this what you want for me?' he will guide us."

I know that there isn't one girl or young man out there that isn't loved and cherished by our Heavenly Father. He gave each of you talents and abilities, maybe more than you even suspect. You have to do your part, prepare, practice, and work. And search for ways to use them. Then wonderful things will happen to you, wonderful things that Heavenly Father has in his plan for you.

Let Your Light So Shine

CHRIS CROWE

Mr. Crowe," moaned a girl from my sophomore English class as she trudged into my room during lunch, "why are you forcing us to do those dumb informative speeches? I haven't been able to think of anything to talk about. Can you give me some good ideas?"

"Sure," I answered. "Why not talk about the extinction of the Jaredites? Or maybe you could tell the class about archeological evidence of the Book of Mormon in South America—"

"I would never do that," she broke in. "Then everyone would know I'm a Mormon!"

"What would be wrong with that?" I asked, teasing.

"It's bad enough already that so many people know."

What a bushel case, I thought. At school, she tries to hide her gospel light under a bushel. That makes it pretty hard to be much of a missionary.

Of course, she doesn't need to advertise her religion with floodlights and speeches on the Jaredites and the Book of Mormon to be a good missionary at school. But she might be a good missionary, maybe even a great missionary, if she would let her light shine—just a little.

I was never a good missionary at school either, until I overcame my fear that my students would discover I was LDS. Since then I've reaped many benefits—more than I had ever imagined.

One year, during paragraph lecture number 177, I noticed someone beckoning to me through the small rectangular window in my classroom door. I stepped out into the hall to see who my visitor was.

"Hi, Mr. Crowe. Remember me?" It was Tracy, a student from a few years past. She hadn't changed much: same blonde hair, same smile, same cheerful countenance. Yes, I remembered her. "Sorry to take you away from your class," she said, "but I just wanted to stop by and thank you for recommending BYU to me."

"Well, that's a relief. I figured you were here to tell me that you hated it."

She laughed.

"So, are you glad you went to a Mormon university?"

Her smile changed to a more serious version, one that I remembered from the after-class conversations a couple years earlier about BYU. She had been curious to know if a nonmember like her would fit into an LDS campus.

"Yes. Things have been going great for me. The university is just as good as you said it would be, but something has happened, something I never expected when I decided to go to BYU." Her smile broadened. "Oh, Mr. Crowe, I never knew I could be so happy. Last week I was baptized!"

She could have knocked me over with a blink. I never dreamed that she would ever have an interest in the Church. As a matter of fact, I wasn't ever sure that she really would attend BYU. But I was glad she did.

"Tracy, that's super! Congratulations." I shook her hand. "But your parents aren't LDS, are they? How are they reacting to this?"

Her expression darkened momentarily. "They aren't real excited about my decision, but they did drive up to Provo for my baptism. I think they realize that I'm old enough to make my own choices; they'll eventually adjust to having a Mormon daughter.

"Well, I won't keep you from your class any longer," she said with a happy shrug of her shoulders. "I just came to thank you for everything, for your part in my conversion to the Church." She turned and walked down the hallway and outside to the parking lot.

I still couldn't believe it. She had said that *I* was partially responsible for her conversion. Why did she think that? All I ever did was talk to her when she felt like talking. When she had questions about BYU or the Church, I answered them, but I never preached to her, gave her a Book of Mormon, or asked her the Golden Questions.

It later dawned on me that I had been doing missionary work without knowing it. I wasn't tramping door to door, riding a bike through blizzards in a foreign land, being chased by hostile mobs, or giving missionary discussions, but I was, in my own way, being a missionary—and I had helped make a difference in someone's life. It was a relief to realize that missionary work didn't have to be painful or unpleasant. Sometimes it was as simple as talking to someone. Tracy's conversion—my first successful missionary experience—showed me how easy it is to share the gospel with nonmembers. All I had to do, all I did, was let Tracy know I was LDS, and she did the rest. Missionary work was never so easy.

With my new outlook on missionary work, it became easier for me to talk openly about the Church. At our end-of-school picnic, for example, another girl, one of our cheerleaders, asked me about the Church.

"Hey, Mr. Crowe," she asked as she sat down next to me, "is it true that you converted to the Mormon Church from the Catholic Church when you were in high school?"

"Yep."

"That's what I had heard. Well, I have this problem. I have a testimony of the Church—I even go to sacrament meeting when my parents will let me—but I'm not allowed to join the Church. My dad thinks I'm being brainwashed by my Mormon friends; he won't let me get baptized until I'm eighteen.

"All the kids at school think I want to get baptized just because I have a Mormon boyfriend. It bothers me that they think he's pressuring me into the Church. What can I do?"

We talked about her frustrations for a while, and I had a chance to share a condensed version of my own struggle to join the Church. "Just hang in there," I told her at the end of our conversation. "Things will work out for you."

On my way home that afternoon I realized that my discussion

with the young cheerleader was my second missionary experience in less than a semester. I had accomplished more missionary work in the past eighteen weeks than I had in the previous five years.

It was encouraging to realize that I really was doing my part to help spread the gospel. For many years I had felt that I was the crummiest member missionary ever allowed into the Church, but finally I discovered a missionary field where I had least expected it—in school.

Those positive missionary experiences made me more willing to let people know that I'm LDS. It wasn't easy at first to peek out from under the bushel where I used to hide my LDS identity while I was at school. But by simply letting others know I was a member of the Church, by letting people catch a glimpse of the light of the gospel, I increased my missionary potential enormously.

We've been told, "Behold the field is white already to harvest" (D&C 4:4). School is a great place to begin that harvest and to spread the light of the gospel. I didn't have to look any further than my English class, and neither, I'll bet, will you.

Family

$\mathscr{A}$ Kidney for David

JOHN BYTHEWAY

One December night at a family Christmas party, my oldest brother, David, asked if he could talk to me. We went into the front room, where he told me that he was sick again. This wasn't just any kind of sick. This was big-time, "I'm going to die if something doesn't change" type of sick. David continued, "It looks like I'm going to need one of your kidneys." Fortunately, all of us are born with a spare kidney. We don't have a spare heart or brain, but we do have a spare kidney. In fact, the body uses only about half of one kidney at any given moment.

Eight years earlier, we had gone to the hospital to prepare for a transplant surgery. They tested everyone in the family to see who had the best match. It was me. But there was a problem: I had just received my mission call. I was to report to the Missionary Training Center within two months. We didn't know what to do. We asked our stake president, and he called the missionary committee of the Church. The problem was explained to Elder Bruce R. McConkie. He considered the situation and finally said, "Send the boy on a mission." So I went. About a month later, I received a letter from David that said, "Hey, everything seems to be okay. My kidneys are fine for now. Have a great mission!" And I did. I learned once again that God knows what he's doing and that he is a God of miracles.

Now, years later, David was sick again. I had a chance to do something for my brother that no one else could do. I had a chance to give, not take. I was honored to do it. I was proud that I had a drug-free, alcohol-free, tobacco-free kidney. When the transplant coordinator came into the hospital room to speak to us, she looked at David and asked, "Are you the recipient?" David said yes. She looked at me and asked, "Are you the donor?" I said yes. She looked at David and said, "In a couple of days, you're going to feel great." Then she looked at me and said, "You will be in a significant amount of pain." I thought to myself, *Boy, she doesn't beat around the bush.* After that, she showed a video called *So, You're Having an Operation.* This video was without question one of the grossest things I had ever seen in my life. Don't rent it! After the video, David and I exchanged glances. We both had that "Gee, this is gonna be fun" look on our faces.

After I had chatted with the surgeon and a man from the National Kidney Foundation, the surgeon handed me a green bottle of antibacterial soap and said, "Get up at 6:30 A.M., take a shower with this stuff, put on these special clothes, and don't go anywhere." I took one look at those special clothes and said, "Believe me, I ain't goin' *anywhere* in those special clothes." Have you ever seen hospital "special clothes"? Whoever designed those gowns has never read *For the Strength of Youth.* They took me at about 7:00 A.M., and I awoke in my room at about 2:30 in the afternoon. My mom was standing at the foot of the bed, and my dad was in fetal position on the floor. This seemed a little odd. Apparently I had been moaning in pain for the past few hours, and my dad (the World War II battle-hardened, aircraft carrier, navy veteran) could hardly stand it. So he curled up in a ball on the floor. Mom, however, was tough. "Hey, I've had six kids, buster; you can't scare me." I remember asking, "How's David?" and then I felt the significant pain the nurse warned me about. Ouch. I felt like my side had been attacked with a samurai sword. *Hoi-chu!*

I looked around the room and saw other members of my family. All were smiling but close to tears. It was a very amazing day. The love and concern and feeling of family were so thick in that room you could cut it with a knife (oooh, bad choice of words). The next day, when I saw David, was one of the best days of my life. He looked so good. (He still does.) I've wondered on occasion why the Lord just didn't heal David when I went on my mission. I know he could have, but I'm glad he didn't because I learned a powerful lesson that I'm making a feeble attempt to share with you now. This whole story was written to prepare you for this sentence. Are you ready? Here it comes: *If you want to be happy in your family, focus on what you can give, not on what you can get.* I had the chance to give something to my brother that only I could give. You too have gifts of love and service that only you can give. Try the experiment! In your family focus more on giving than on getting, and watch how you change inside, and how the spirit in your home changes. And just for fun, do a few things anonymously. To alter an old phrase, "Ask not what your family can do for you, but what you can do for your family." If I could bring my family that close together again, I'd consider giving another major body part.

"Come On, Lou!"

JACK R. CHRISTIANSON

When I was a senior in high school, I was sometimes embarrassed to have my mom come to my ball games because she was so loud. She would always scream at the top of her lungs, "Come on, Lou! You can do it, Lou! That's my boy!" I was mortified. My dad usually wouldn't sit by her because he was embarrassed. He would always find a reason to move. He would come to the sideline or to the dugout; he would buy popcorn or a drink. She didn't care. She would sit toward the top of the stands so she could stand up. Whenever I did anything noteworthy, or when I was about to come to bat, she always let me and everyone else know that I could do whatever needed to be done.

Then one spring afternoon my feelings changed. It was an intense baseball game. Our team was behind the entire game until we scored four runs in the last inning. Finally, at the end of regulation play the score was tied. The game went into extra innings, and the other team scored two runs. When we finally got them out, we all gathered in the dugout and vowed that we wouldn't lose and that no one would strike out. (I could talk real big because I was the sixth batter up. I didn't think I'd get a chance to make any difference.)

The first two batters struck out. We then somehow managed to score two runs to tie the score again. It was a Roy Hobbs–Kurt Gibson moment. I came to the plate with two outs, one man on base, and the score tied in extra innings. This was something I had dreamed about all my life. I had a chance to be the hero or the goat.

As I walked to the plate, butterflies were swarming in the pit of my stomach! My hands were sweating, and my heart was almost in the batter's box, when my mother stood up and screamed, "Come on, Lou! You can do it, Lou. You can do it! That's my boy!" I wanted to hide behind the umpire.

I looked at her with a glare that said, "Please don't do this to me. Please love me enough to be quiet." It didn't work. I hoped that my dad would sense my discomfort and, just this once, get Mom to sit down and be quiet. But Dad had found some other errand in the park; he wasn't anywhere near her.

I battled the pitcher to a full count, three balls and two strikes. The intensity couldn't have been greater in a movie! I battled and battled. Two strikes, two outs, one man on base. I could bring in the winning run. After several foul balls, the opposing coach called time-out. He signaled to the bull pen, and one of the star relief pitchers trotted to the mound. All he had to do was throw one strike and the game would be over.

All during the new pitcher's warm-up, my mother was yelling that I didn't need to worry. That was easy for her to say; she didn't have to try to hit that little white dot.

The umpire finally signaled us to play ball. Now *I* called a time-out and used the break to hit my cleats with the bat. I didn't really think about why I did that. I had seen Reggie Jackson do it in many tight situations, so I did it. Then I dug my right foot into the ground and touched the end of the bat to the corner of the plate, and my mom yelled again, "Come on, Lou. You can do it, Lou!"

I was so frustrated that I stepped out of the box and glared at her in disgust. She glared back with her fists clenched and shaking in my direction. I don't know what happened at that moment, but my relationship with that dear woman has never been the same since. I realized, for the first time in my young eighteen years, that my mother loved me so much that she wasn't afraid of making a fool of herself in front of the entire crowd in order to show me.

I felt the adrenaline pump through my system. I knew I was going to hit that ball. I was going to show my mom that I could do it! And yes, I was her boy and proud of it!

I stepped into the box with a newfound confidence, looking for an inside fast ball. For some reason the pitcher threw me a slow-breaking curve ball. It had my name on it! As it broke I crunched it down the left-field line. It had enough on it to be a home run. But it went foul!

Talk about pressure! Now I was going to swing, no matter what. If the ball went twenty feet high, I'd throw the bat at it. I was going to hit that ball.

The pitcher wound up and let it rip. It was the same pitch. I couldn't believe it. I waited a split second longer than I had before, and then made solid contact. I still remember standing at home plate, my arms raised in triumph, as I watched the ball sail over the left center-field fence. I proudly trotted around the bases, knowing I was the hero.

But what happened as I came to home plate floored me. There, in the middle of my ecstatic teammates, was my mother. I don't know how she got there so quickly without throwing her back out, but there she was, jumping up and down and screaming.

After all the hoopla at home plate, she grabbed me and twirled me around, all the time kissing me and whispering, "I knew you could do it, son. I knew you could do it."

Then she humbled me to tears. As I remember it, she said, "But son, I'd love you even if you had struck out." And I knew she did.

My picture was taken for the town newspaper, the crowd soon was gone, and being a hero for a few minutes became a pleasant memory. But my relationship with my mother had changed forever. From that day to this, I can honestly say I don't remember one disrespectful, rude, or ornery word escaping my lips to that woman. She and my dad have become two of my greatest heroes. Oh, I'm aware of many of their weaknesses, and I know they are far from being perfect. But I am convinced that the reason why I love them so deeply today is that they first loved me.

Perhaps not everyone who reads this story has been blessed

to have a mother like mine, or even to have a mother at all. But that is not the point. The point is, if we are going to be loved, we must learn to love first. We must discover this life-changing power to love ourselves, our neighbors, and most of all our God.

$\mathscr{I}$ Decided I Had Better Start Hating My Parents

BRAD WILCOX

I loved my parents until I entered seventh grade. Then I found out it wasn't cool to love your parents. I remember hearing other students talk about how mean, unfair, and old-fashioned their parents were, and I decided that if I planned to survive in this new environment, I had better start hating my parents. So I hated them. It wasn't as easy as I first thought, because I really loved them, but a man's gotta do what a man's gotta do.

All the way home on the bus, I tried to hate them. All the way up my long driveway, I told myself I hated them. I flopped down in front of the TV and reminded myself to hate them. But you just can't hate your mom and dad when you're watching *The Brady Bunch*. I decided to go outside to the field behind my house. *Outdoors is the proper place to hate parents,* I said to myself knowingly.

Between my house and the field was a barbed-wire fence. All my life I had gone under the fence, but now, being a man, I determined to go over the fence. I grabbed the top of the rough wooden fence post with my right hand and began climbing the barbed wire until I straddled the fence with one leg on each side. At that moment I thought, *This is about the dumbest thing I've ever done.* Suddenly, the barbed wire on which I was balancing gave out. I landed forcefully on the fence, and the jagged wooden post shot through my right hand—yes, in one side and out the other. Believe me, my first thought was not *I hate my parents.* I began yelling for my mom and dad as loudly as I could. I did not care if they were at the South Pole, they were going to hear me!

My dad was driving up the driveway. He heard me screaming and rushed to the fence. He pulled my hand off the post, wrapped it in a dish towel, and hurried me to the hospital emergency room. Not once did I think, *I can't stand this guy. He doesn't like my music. He doesn't like my hair.* Not once did I think, *I am going to be so embarrassed if any of my friends see me with my dad.* And I sure didn't think, *My dad is so old-fashioned to still believe in emergency rooms!* On the contrary, I felt grateful that my dad was there and was willing to help me when I got myself into such a ridiculous mess.

The entire time the doctor stitched my right hand back together, my dad sat next to me, holding my left hand and squeezing it over and over. I'll never forget the love I felt from my dad that day—the very day I had decided I was going to hate him.

That day I found out just how important it is to be friends with your parents.

Old Blue and the New Firebird

R. SCOTT SIMMONS

One day my mom cut a picture of a shiny red Firebird out of a magazine and put it on the bulletin board. When I asked her about it, she commented that one day she was going to have one just like it. At the time she was driving "Old Blue," an old beat-up Chevy that we had put back together several times with baling wire and duct tape.

It was not long until we had saved enough money to replace Old Blue. It did not take Mom long to find a car like the one in her picture. The only problem was that it was out of our price range. After a week of trying to figure out how to pay for it, Mom finally decided her dream car would have to wait.

However, the next day Dad came home driving the new Firebird. You can imagine how thrilled and surprised my mom was to see her dream car. I'll never forget my dad's response when I questioned him about being able to afford the car. He said, "Son, look how it makes your mom feel to have a new car. I would have paid twice that much for her to feel that way."

$\mathcal{P}$lease Bring Us Home

JANNA DeVORE

About fifteen miles north of Elko, Nevada, is a stretch of highway dotted with signs warning motorists not to pick up hitchhikers because of a prison facility nearby. To four college students traveling from Provo, Utah, to San Francisco, these signs were a bit unsettling. My roommates and I were glad to cruise by them on our way to California's Bay Area for Thanksgiving weekend. We didn't think twice about the signs until four days later on our way back to Provo. It was then that our car suddenly stopped precisely ten yards to the north of one of those ominous blue signs.

Our first instincts were to flag down another car and ask for a ride back to Elko. But images of escaped convicts kept us locked inside the car. It was four in the afternoon, it was snowing, and it would definitely be dark and very cold within the hour. We needed help fast but were too afraid to even get out of the car. We offered a short prayer, and thirty minutes later a man driving a snowplow stopped and radioed the police for us. A young officer piled us into his car, called a tow truck, and dropped us off at a motel in Elko.

We soon got over our fears and realized how blessed we were to get off the highway unharmed and be in a safe, warm motel room. Our only problem now was getting back to Provo. Each of us dialed home collect, expecting that our parents would wire money for bus tickets or a rental car. We were surprised when each set of parents immediately offered to drive to Elko and get us.

Even for the closest set of parents, this meant a three-hour drive to Elko and a four-hour drive back to Provo. It meant disrupting work schedules and finding baby-sitters for the other children. Eventually we decided that it would be best for Jenni's mom and grandpa to drive down to get us. Relieved, we went to bed and expected to see Jenni's mom by noon the next day.

Things didn't go quite as planned. Overnight the snowstorm had worsened, and the roads were terrible. Despite leaving Salt Lake City at 10:00 A.M. Jenni's mom didn't get to us until four that afternoon. The roads back were equally icy, and a typically four-hour drive took six hours. Still, Jenni's mom and grandpa never uttered a word of complaint during the entire drive home. They were only happy to help and grateful that we would be home soon.

No matter where we had been stranded, any of our parents would have done all they could to bring us back home. The same is true of our heavenly parents. And our Heavenly Father will take us all the way home, not just to a safe resting place. No matter how lost or confused we may be, we need only to make a humble call to our Heavenly Father, promising to heed His words, and He will lead us back.

Unfortunately, our earthly parents may not always be at the other end of the line when we call. Many parents cannot or will not answer their children's cries. As I rode home from Elko in the safe confines of a warm van, I realized just how much my parents love me. Even more, I knew that my Heavenly Father would always help me. He does so without complaint, for He is happy just to know that I am on my way home and will soon be safe in His arms.

$\mathcal{M}$arci's Proposal

CARLOS E. ASAY

$\mathbf{M}$arci reverenced her parents. That is why she sought their counsel soon after she had received a marriage proposal from a young man. The two had dated at college for several months and they seemed to have much in common. Both were religious; both loved children; and both loved the Lord. Her suitor had professed his love and good intentions. Marci wasn't so sure.

Mother and Dad were not able at the time to visit Marci at school, where the proposal could have been discussed at length. But they promised to fast and pray over the matter before sharing their advice. Their love for Marci was deep and abiding. No parents had ever raised a more obedient daughter than she.

A few days later, Marci's parents called her back on the telephone. Their response was simply: "We have prayed and pondered over your proposal and we don't have a good feeling. We cannot tell you why these feelings have been so negative. Moreover, we are reluctant to judge the young man because we have never met him. But we don't think that you should accept the engagement ring."

Though temporarily disappointed with the response from her mother and father, Marci trusted their feelings and accepted their counsel without argument and ended the courtship. There was no debate, no crying, and no appeal for additional consideration. She trusted implicitly in her parents' word, knowing that it had been spoken in love and out of the deepest concern for her well-being.

Later, Marci's father wrote:

Marci, I remind you that you are a very special young lady. Your body is clean, your mind pure, and your spirit strong. Therefore, be very cautious in all your dealings. Don't permit anyone to stain your soul or mar your character. Although at times you may get lonely or wonder if that knight in shining armor will ever arrive, I assure you that he will in due time. Consider it this way: The reason he (the knight) is taking so long is that he is strengthening and polishing his armor. When it is sufficiently prepared, he will come and claim you his. You see, this added time of waiting is given to you and him as a time of preparation. Consequently, both of you will be far better equipped to fight the battles of life and to protect the children that will bless your relationship.

Just be patient, prayerful and clean. Trust the Lord and he will extend his blessings in due time. We love you, dear. Our hopes, wishes, and desires are only for your eternal happiness. God bless you always.

A few months later "Mr. Right" came upon the scene. He took Marci to the temple, where they were sealed together for time and for all eternity. In the years that have followed, Marci has testified concerning this important, scripture-based fact: Loving parents do not chasten or give advice after their own pleasures; they do it for the profit of the children so that the children might be partakers of holiness and happiness (see Hebrews 12:10).

Family Loyalty

MATTHEW O. RICHARDSON

One day I was playing tennis with two of my older brothers and my sister at a park near our home. To fully understand this story, however, it is important to know that my sister is one of the most sensitive human beings on earth. She is the type of individual who wears her emotions on her sleeve. There were three tennis courts side-by-side, and each court was enclosed by a chain-link fence. This kept the balls from rolling between the three courts. My two older brothers were on one side of the net, and my sister and I were playing on the opposite side.

Playing on the court next to ours were two young men who were about the same age as my sister. They were loud boys and filled with comments that were not very appropriate. Unfortunately, they directed some of their inappropriate comments toward my sister. When my sister heard what those boys had said, she started crying right on the spot. She stood there weeping when she should be returning a serve. Not realizing what had taken place, but fully realizing we had just lost the point, I asked her, "What happened to you?" My sister just stood sobbing in the middle of the tennis court.

Then I heard a *cling-cling* noise. As I turned around, I realized that the noise was made by the gate in the fence between the two tennis courts as it slammed shut. I looked across the net and found that my two older brothers were no longer there. You see, not only did these two young men say their rude comments loud enough for my sister to hear—they were loud enough for my two older brothers to hear as well. By the time I figured out what was happening, my two brothers were already on those boys' tennis court.

I ran through the gate to join my brothers. By the time I arrived, my oldest brother was sitting on top of one of those young men and had his tennis racket across the guy's throat. I looked over to the other side of the court, and there was my other brother, who had taken hold of the other boy and was doing what I call the "chain-link bounce." He had the boy by the shirt and would toss him against the chain-link fence. The boy would bounce off the fence and back into the clutches of my brother. My brother kept repeating the process.

As I watched this spectacle unfold, I heard one of my brothers say: "*Nobody*"—and he was adamant about this—"*Nobody* says those things about my sister." I remember listening to my brother and the first thing that came to my mind was, *Wait a minute. I heard you say almost the same thing to her at home—just last night! How does this work?* You see, I guess I grew up in a pretty normal family. We had our differences as well as our strengths—like most families.

But I discovered something very important on the tennis court that day, a lesson I have not since forgotten. At that point in my life, I knew that if someone was going to mess with one Richardson, that person would have to take on *all* Richardsons. Despite what happened between my brother and sister before, a casual argument or disagreement once in a while, there was an understanding that nobody could say certain things to our family members—nobody! I would hope that still holds true for my family today, although we're grown and have homes of our own. One Richardson stands up for all Richardsons. I know that in my home, with my children, that rule holds true for my family.

Please don't misunderstand. I'm certainly not advocating physical intimidation or violence towards those outside my family circle as a means to promote family unity. I'm simply saying that there is something magnificent that happens to a family where you find loyalty. When spouse stands up for spouse, siblings stand up for siblings, children stand up for parents, and parents stand strong for children, this builds a loyalty that gives families deep-inside strength. Family loyalty is a strong sense of belonging that nobody can take away—nobody!

The Stick-Together Families

EDGAR A. GUEST

The stick-together families are happier by far
Than the brothers and the sisters who take separate highways are.
The gladdest people living are the wholesome folks who make
A circle at the fireside that no power but death can break.
And the finest of conventions ever held beneath the sun
Are the little family gatherings when the busy day is done.

There are rich folk, there are poor folk, who imagine they are
    wise,
And they're very quick to shatter all the little family ties.
Each goes searching after pleasure in his own selected way,
Each with strangers likes to wander, and with strangers likes to
    play.
But it's bitterness they harvest, and it's empty joy they find,
For the children that are wisest are the stick-together kind.

There are some who seem to fancy that for gladness they must
    roam,
That for smiles that are the brightest they must wander far from
    home.
That the strange friend is the true friend, and they travel far astray
And they waste their lives in striving for a joy that's far away,
But the gladdest sort of people, when the busy day is done,
Are the brothers and the sisters who together share their fun.

It's the stick-together family that wins the joys of earth,
That hears the sweetest music and that finds the finest mirth;

It's the old home roof that shelters all the charm that life can give;
There you find the gladdest play-ground, there the happiest spot
    to live.
And, O weary, wandering brother, if contentment you would win,
Come you back unto the fireside and be comrade with your kin.

Learning Positive Lessons from Negative Examples

BRAD WILCOX

A boy I'll call Mike grew up with a dictatorial father he felt he could not please. Mike was continually being compared with his brothers and coming up short. It seemed that nothing he did was good enough for his father. To make matters worse, Mike's father had a sharp temper, and any disagreement usually ended in a heavy-handed whipping.

As Mike grew up he made several promises to himself that when he had children of his own he would not repeat his father's mistakes. Mike determined that although he could not change what had happened with his father in the past, he could learn from the experiences. Coming from a dysfunctional home did not mean he had to be dysfunctional himself.

Mike served a mission, married in the temple, had children, and remained true to his private promises made as a teenager. Mike was sensitive to his children's feelings. He accepted their individual differences and did not compare them with each other. He praised positive behavior, and when a child's behavior was not so positive, he talked to that child privately rather than exploding in front of everyone as his father had done. Remembering how he craved approval and affection as a child, he hugged and kissed his own children daily and attended one child's musical concerts as often as he attended another's sports events.

Now, many years later, children and grandchildren who have been blessed by Mike's good example are thankful he learned so much from a bad one. Mike explained, "I think the essence of honoring dishonorable parents is to let any cycle of negative behavior stop with you. That's what I tried to do. It hasn't always been easy, but when I felt sorry for myself it helped to look around and see that others were also dealing with less-than-perfect family circumstances. I knew many people who were remaining active in the Church, fulfilling callings, attending to their duties, and finding a great deal of joy in their lives despite their parents' problems."

Just as Mike did, those in negative situations at home can still learn positive lessons.

No one in dysfunctional family circumstances would ever wish the same on another soul. Still, there can be great comfort in knowing that others who have had to deal with similar trials have survived. As we seek to learn, we can draw strength and courage from their experiences.

Gospel
Lessons

Motorcycle Helmets, Sisters, and the Holy Ghost

TODD MURDOCK

In the summer before my high school senior year, I purchased a motorcycle. Red and shiny, it was the first vehicle I ever owned. Along with the bike came a helmet which I was instructed to always wear. I no longer had desires to die, so I was obedient. I loved to ride. I had a friend who loved to ride his bike with me, and together we covered many miles on our sleek machines.

Summer also meant football, and practices twice a day. One day after practice, I decided to ride over to my friend's house, and then together we'd go to a local church to shoot baskets, working out bruises encountered during the day. Because the distance to his house was short I decided not to wear my helmet.

My bike was parked in the driveway, screaming for me to come and ride. Again I was obedient. As I swung my leg over the seat and sat down, I heard in my mind, "Put your helmet on." The impression was so strong that I got off the bike. I thought for sure I was talking to myself.

I sat down again the second time. Again I heard, "Put your helmet on." "No way," I thought. "I'm talking to myself." I stood up again the second time, promising I wouldn't talk to myself.

I shook my hands, took a deep breath, and then sat down. For the third time the voice came back. This time I heard my name. "Todd, put your helmet on."

I was amazed! "OK, I'm going to play along," I thought. "I'm going crazy, but I'll play along just in case this really is the Holy Ghost."

I then determined that in my effort of obedience I would ask my sister to run downstairs to my bedroom and retrieve my helmet for me. If she would do this, then I would wear the helmet; if not, I had done everything in my power to be obedient and the Lord would have to take care of me.

I walked back to the house, stuck my head in the front door, and asked my sister to get my helmet. I knew she wouldn't. We were at war with each other. At this time in our lives we had undertaken the tasks of making each other as miserable as possible. A simple favor from either one of us to the other was out of the question. In addition to this matter of our wars, she was now watching her favorite TV show, *Days of Our Lives,* and I knew she would not part from it for me.

As soon as I asked, however, she jumped up, ran to the basement and into my room, came back with my helmet, handed it to me, then sat back down in front of the TV.

Inexpressible confusion filled my soul! "This isn't my sister," I thought, "this is the angel Moroni in disguise." Nevertheless I had my helmet, so I put it on and went on my way.

Second North in Kaysville, heading west, will take you under the overpass, over the railroad tracks, and then it's wide open road. An open road is an incredible stimulus for young teenagers to open the throttle on their bike and cruise. I did this, passing farmers' fields quite rapidly. I was alive, it felt great, it was me.

The road eventually intersects, and I slowed down to make a right-hand turn. Still no traffic, and I raced down the road again. However, the road did not continue in a straight line. It curved around an oak tree growing in the yard of a local farmer. Approaching the curve, I slowed down but wanted to take the turn as fast as I could. One of the joys of motorcycle riding is to lean the heavy bike and see how close you can come to the ground without wiping out. If you wipe out you've leaned too far.

I began my turn, and as I cornered at the top of the curve the farmer backed his truck out of his driveway and into my lane. I didn't see him until then because of the oak tree. I straightened the bike up to go around him in his lane, but he gunned his truck to get out of my lane.

It's a sickening feeling to know you're going to crash. I locked up my brakes and braced myself for the collision. It never happened. The blur of the truck flashed by in my peripheral vision as I headed for tall grass on the side of the road. It was slick but I felt I could keep things under control.

Suddenly the bike stopped and I went flying straight into the air. I could see the bike below me, and I thought, "Hmph, I'm flying straight in the air." Then, because my intelligence level is so high, I thought, "Hmph, I'm going to come down." Sure enough I did. I was heading for the ground head first, and a thought raced through my mind suggesting that I duck my head as if I were to hit someone in football practice. (Because of the circumstances I was unable to call a time-out to discuss other options.) I ducked my head and hit the ground. It was the best hit I'd ever had! The impact was absorbed in my head, neck, and shoulders, and I somersaulted gently onto my back.

The farmer stopped his truck, jumping out to see if I was OK. I assured him arrogantly that I was absolutely fine, almost acting as if I actually had fun flying through the air and landing on my head. I felt very weak. Eventually, I picked up my bike and headed for home.

As I walked in the front door my sister sensed something was wrong. I told her I'd been in an accident. Overly concerned, she told me to lie down and rest and wait for Mom to come home. I did this, then shared the experience with my mother as she listened sitting on the edge of my bed. I mentioned the "voice" that prompted me to put my helmet on. After I had finished, Mom pointed out that it was the Holy Ghost that had saved my life that day.

Reflecting on that experience I believe that I did talk to myself. I believe that I'm the one who said, "Put on your helmet." I also believe the Holy Ghost inspired me. Let me explain. As I sat on my motorcycle I felt impressed to do something. My mind searched to verbalize the impression. When I told myself to put my helmet on, that thought coincided with the impression and I knew what I was supposed to do. So what I really did was verbalize the impression in my mind. My mind and heart had the same answer, which is how the Holy Ghost works.

The Obstacle Course

VICKEY PAHNKE

As we allow the Savior to help us, we can rise above this murky, dimly lit world. Immersing yourself in the scriptures can transport you, at least momentarily, out of your difficulties, your hurts. You will feel the protective influence of the Holy Ghost to safeguard against unrighteous, dangerous influences or situations. You will be lifted to a higher place where you will feel more peaceful, more positively directed. Christ heals broken hearts, tends burdened souls. His love radiates from the words of the scriptures. The more familiar we become with his teachings, the less we will experience malfunction. As we read, it's not that the obstacle course of life becomes easier; but *we* become better at listening for divine direction, learning to steer clear of detours that would throw us off course.

I know of a ward that maybe is much like your own. It has a huge youth group. Jenni, a beautiful young woman, is a member of this ward. She loves the gospel, loves to get involved in activities with her friends, and is pretty much like you and me. Except that Jenni is blind. There are sometimes activities planned that she cannot participate in, and others that make her feel awkward or left out.

On one occasion the young women planned a special activity with their fathers. In preparation, an obstacle course was set up in the cultural hall, complete with tires, sawhorses, and so on. The object would be for the girls, beginning at one end of the hall, to make it to their fathers at the other end. One by one, each receiving instruction from her dad, they would move through this course. The equalizing factor was that each girl would be blindfolded. Jenni needn't feel left out, and it would be fun for all participating.

It must have been a hilarious night. Fathers were getting frustrated; daughters were getting agitated and falling all over the place. On the sidelines the others were shouting instructions and contradicting one another. Laughter filled the hall. Not one girl was getting through the course.

Jenni was last up. A quiet came over the hall as she stood ready for her turn. The other girls had whipped off their blindfolds. Jenni would not have the luxury of seeing this room when the games were over.

Her father quietly said: "Jenni, listen to me. Don't pay attention to what anyone else says, just listen to my voice. I will guide you through."

Jenni began her trip. Among those watching, eyes widened in amazement as she carefully maneuvered. Once or twice she stopped, got her bearings, had her dad repeat his instructions, before she moved forward. Jaws dropped as Jenni continued—never falling, never losing her composure. In time she made it to the other end and into the arms of her father, who swung her around as the others clapped and encircled the "winners."

"No way!" "Incredible!" The girls crowded around Jenni, amazed at how easily she had gotten through the course that they had failed to navigate. "How did you do it?"

"It was easy," Jenni said. "I just listened to my father's voice and did what he told me to do."

Jenni taught a powerful lesson that night.

My young friends, this life is a real obstacle course. There are unexpected turns and pitfalls everywhere. People on the sidelines often shout instructions, many times simultaneously giving different directions. It gets confusing. It is treacherous. And it is easy to fall.

Jenni gave us the advice we need. At the end of this life's course our Father in Heaven waits with outstretched arms. We must remember to listen to his voice and do what he tells us to do. Listening to the voices all around us cannot ensure our safety. But if we tune into his instructions we can make it back home.

$\mathcal{H}$onoring the Priesthood

ALLAN K. BURGESS AND MAX H. MOLGARD

Just two weeks after Alan received the Aaronic Priesthood, he learned his first lesson on the importance of that priesthood. He was sitting on the front row, waiting to pass the sacrament, when he and some of the other deacons started poking each other, laughing, flipping rubber bands, and making a general nuisance of themselves. Alan's dad watched from several benches back, and it didn't take long before he decided that he needed to teach his son a lesson. He quietly walked up the aisle, grabbed Alan and one of his friends by their ears, and escorted them down the aisle toward the door. As they walked down the aisle on tiptoe, Alan noticed a red-faced lady and realized it was his mother. He had never seen her look this way before. It was not the kind of look you see on a mother's face when she is proud of her son.

When the trio got to the foyer, Alan's dad told him that if he wanted to act like a child he would treat him like one. He put Alan over his knee and gave him a spanking. Alan's friend thought sure he would be next, but instead he was told that his father would be informed if such mischief ever happened again. Alan's dad then concluded this foyer lesson with the advice that if the two boys were going to participate in priesthood duties they should do so with honor and dignity.

Alan remembered this lesson well until he was ordained a teacher. As a teacher he had the responsibility of preparing the sacrament before the Sunday meetings. One day while he was filling the water trays, another teacher came in and threw some water in his face. Alan immediately threw a cup of water back at him.

With this, war began. The other boy squirted Alan with the little hose they used to fill the cups, and then ran. Alan filled a small bucket with water and went after him. As the other boy tried to open a door to escape, Alan let the water go. The target ducked just at the right instant—a counselor from another ward's bishopric walked directly into the airborne stream, which hit him right in the face.

Alan just stood looking in total shock. As the water ran down the counselor's face, he grabbed Alan by the arm and escorted him to the bishop's office. The bishop, in turn, marched him to his dad. When Alan's dad learned what had happened, Alan saw a look of disappointment and hurt on his dad's face that he would never forget. Alan again resolved to honor the priesthood.

However, the lesson that really taught Alan what the priesthood was all about came from a man whose name was Pete. Pete had been Alan's deacons quorum adviser and had shown a lot of love and concern for him. But Pete was elderly and crippled now. He had to use two canes to walk and was constantly in pain.

One Sunday Alan was the only priest at the sacrament table. Seeing this, Pete hobbled up to the table to assist him. Alan said the blessing on the bread perfectly, reading the words from a card. He had always been proud of the fact that he could say the prayer with such precision.

Then a great lesson on honoring the priesthood was taught to Alan by his elderly companion at the sacrament table. As Pete knelt to bless the water, he struggled in pain to get his legs to bend so that he could get down on both knees. Many of the priests had knelt on only one knee, but it was obvious Pete had made up *his* mind that if he was going to use the priesthood, he was going to use it right. When Pete was ready to begin, Alan handed him the prayer card. Pete said, "Thank you," and then set the card aside. Alan listened as Pete spoke the prayer from his heart rather than from a card.

Alan would never forget the stillness that settled over the congregation as Pete said that prayer. The Holy Ghost descended on the people there that day, and many were moved to tears. Pete said the same words that had always been said, but the difference was that he really spoke to Heavenly Father. Alan noticed that the whole congregation worshipped during the passing of the sacrament that day like never before.

Alan was never able to kneel at the sacrament table after that experience without remembering Pete and his reverence for the priesthood. Alan learned that day that when we honor the priesthood we help not only ourselves but many others as well.

The Power of the Word

R. SCOTT SIMMONS

I didn't get married until I was a little bit older, so when I turned twenty-six and became a menace to society I began to worry a little that my wife had been killed in the War in Heaven and that we would never meet. I hadn't been dating much at the time and was walking across campus one day when I ran into a young woman that I had taught in the MTC and who was now home from her mission. We visited for a minute, and I said, "You know, boy, I'd really like to take you out." Well, she actually said yes, and so she gave me her address and we set up a time to go out. *Man, this is really going to be great!* I thought.

Now, during college I drove a '64 Chevy pickup truck that was totally rusted out. I think it was white, but I'm not sure if it was white with spots of rust or rust with spots of white. Anyhow, it was bad. It was so rusted out that the front quarter panels flapped when I drove down the road. It was also great because the steering was pretty much shot. I could throw the steering wheel from side to side and the truck would go straight down the road. It was a great truck! Everyone loved it. We called it the White Knight. I mean, it was just a classic truck, and it was fun to have. It also had a leak in the manifold and it didn't go very fast, and so everywhere I went people could hear me coming.

Well, I went to pick up my date and pulled into the parking lot at her apartment complex and was a little taken aback because she lived in one of the nicest complexes in all of Provo. I may be overexaggerating, but it seemed so much nicer than my complex. It seemed like every car in the parking lot was a Lexus, a BMW, or a Porche. I got out of my truck and walked up to her door. Her roommate let me in. The apartment was just beautiful, and I remember that they had a chandelier. I would've been happy to have a light with a string. Anyhow, she came downstairs and we walked outside and headed over toward the cars, and then she asked the dumbest of all dumb questions: "Which one's yours?"

"Well," I said somewhat hesitantly, "it's the truck." And she immediately got all excited: "Oh! I love it!"

"Will you marry me?" I wanted to say.

We got in the truck and headed off on our date, and she was really great. She asked if the truck was all original. "Yeah, it's original," I said. She must have thought it was an antique, which I guess it was. But for me it was simply a mode of transportation. She loved the steering wheel, and we had a fun date—one of the most fun dates I'd been on. So naturally when we came back I stumbled through "Boy, I really had a good time" and "I'd really like to see you again." She thought that would be okay, but warned me that she would be out of town until the end of the week, but to call her then.

Now, use your imagination. I'm twenty-six and I'm not married and I'm desperate, and so all week long I have these dreams about a huge field and me running across it into her arms. I was so excited. I didn't, however, want her to think I was anxious, so I waited until Sunday night to call her. And I then arranged a date for the following Wednesday night. She was really nice and very kind and accepted.

On Tuesday night I had just gotten up from saying my prayers when the phone rang. I picked it up, and it was this young woman. *Cool,* I thought. *This is looking good—now she's calling me.*

And then she said, "Hey, listen, the reason I'm calling is that I can't go out on Wednesday night."

"Oh, that's not a problem," I mumbled. "How about Friday night?"

"Oh, you know, I can't go out on Friday night either," she replied.

"Oh, that's okay. How about Saturday?"

Nope.

"Sunday for the fireside? . . . Easter weekend? . . ."

And then she dropped it on me: "Ya know, well, I don't think we should ever go out again."

I just put the phone down and looked for the nearest sharp object and cut my chest open and pulled out my heart and threw it on the floor and stomped on it. Honestly, it hurt. It really hurt.

And then I started to play the "What's the matter with me?" game. I started to think of all the things that I could've done better or different. I was lying there on my bed, just hurting and thinking, *What am I gonna do?* when I remember thinking, *I'll say a prayer.* So I rolled out of my bed, said a prayer, and got back in my bed. I still hurt.

Eventually I looked over at my dresser and saw my Book of Mormon. I reached over and grabbed it and just happened to open to Jacob 3. I read verses 1 and 2: "But behold, I, Jacob, would speak unto you that are pure in heart." (I would never pretend to be pure in heart, but I'm sure trying hard. I think if I would want anyone to say anything about me, that's what I would want them to say—that I'm pure in heart. I continued to read.) "Look unto God with firmness of mind, and pray unto him with exceeding faith, and he will console you in your afflictions, and he will plead your cause, and send down justice upon those who seek your destruction." (Now, think about the iron rod leading to the tree of life and the love of God as you read this next line.) "O all ye that are pure in heart, lift up your heads and receive the pleasing word of God, and feast upon his love; for ye may, if your minds are firm, forever."

Honestly, in that moment it felt as if two of the biggest arms I've ever felt came down and gave me the biggest hug I think I've ever had. I remember closing my scriptures, getting into bed, and immediately falling asleep and never thinking about this thing again. That's the power of the word. That's what happens when you feel God's love.

The Key to Spirituality

BARBARA BARRINGTON JONES

I recall a time when I was in Mexico with Elder and Sister Robert E. Wells giving firesides. I had learned to speak Spanish while growing up on the border in El Paso, Texas, and now I was having the chance to use that language as I gave my talks.

One morning I was sitting outside working on a talk I was to give for Education Days. I had been assigned the topic of keeping in tune with the Spirit. Elder Wells was sitting nearby, and I debated whether I should ask him for help. I finally decided to go over and bother him.

"I'm sorry to bother you," I said, "but I'm doing this talk on keeping in tune with the Spirit. Could you give me one or two little pointers?"

Elder Wells smiled and said: "You know, one time we had a meeting of General Authorities at which one of them gave his formula for keeping in tune with the Spirit. I don't think he'd mind if I shared it with you."

I was excited. A General Authority's formula! I had my paper and pencil ready to write. And what he said was so simple: "The key to all spirituality is the Savior. Fill your mind with thoughts of the Savior. Fill your heart with love for the Savior. Fill your life with service."

$\mathcal{H}$ow to Know How to Know

CHRIS CROWE

I was trapped.

At eighteen, I knew the Church was true. I knew the Lord knew I knew. I knew the missionaries knew I knew. I knew my parents didn't know I knew. And, to make things worse, I didn't know what to do.

It took me three weeks to work up the courage to tell Mom about it. I didn't dare tell Dad because I knew he'd flip.

"Mom," I asked after she recovered from the shock of hearing that her Catholic son wanted to become her Mormon son, "how can I tell Dad?"

She was silent for a moment. "I don't know if you should. Maybe it would be better if I tell him somehow."

"But, Mom, that's not my only problem. I've also got to decide when to get baptized. If I get baptized now, I don't know how Dad will react. But the missionaries think I should get baptized as soon as possible."

"Well, I think you should wait until you go to college," she said. "That's only in a couple of months. Then you'll be away from your father, and he'll have time to make the adjustment before he sees you again. It really would be much easier on both of you if you waited until you were away from home."

I knew she was right, but I wasn't sure if putting off baptism was the right thing to do. So I asked the Elders.

"It's your decision," said Elder Wimpey when I explained my situation to him, "but I'd advise you to get baptized now while you've still got the understanding and guidance of the Spirit. Who knows what might happen if you wait until you're at college?

"But the only way to know for sure when to get baptized," he said as he patted my shoulder, "is to fast and pray about it. Remember that scripture in James? 'If any of you lack wisdom, let him ask of God, that giveth to all men liberally, and upbraideth not; and it shall be given him.' If you'll ask him, the Lord will let you know what he wants you to do."

I had never fasted or prayed in my life, but I was willing to give it a try. For two days my stomach growled and my head ached, and at every possible chance I prayed about what I should do. I made lists of pros and cons. I talked it over with the Elders, my friends, and my mom. And I prayed some more.

Finally, near the end of my second day of prayer and fasting, I had a feeling, a strong feeling, that I should get baptized as soon as possible. I didn't want to get baptized then because I knew it would cause hardships in my family, but I couldn't shake that feeling. I prayed some more. The feeling became stronger. I knew I had to get baptized.

I told the Elders. I told my friends. And I even found the courage to tell Mom and Dad. It wasn't easy, and it wasn't pleasant, but I had confidence that I was doing what the Lord wanted me to do.

Dad didn't say anything when I first told him I was going to be baptized. He just stared at the floor with his face turning red and his feet shuffling uncomfortably. He was too upset to speak. But the next night he did something he'd never done before—he came up to my room to talk with me. I knew he was going to yell.

But he surprised me.

"Son," he said after he had walked in and sat down on my brother's bed, "I want you to know that I think you're making a serious mistake by joining the Mormon Church. I don't want you to do it, but you're old enough now to be able to do what you think is best. When I was your age, I was allowed to do what I thought was right, and I guess I turned out okay." He stood up to leave.

"Dad," I said. "Believe me, I'm sorry that you don't feel good about my joining the Church. But I've thought about it—prayed about it—and I know it's what I've got to do. I'll be okay, I know it."

Then Dad did something else he hadn't done since I was a little kid: he hugged me.

I was baptized the next week, one month before I left for college.

In my first week at college I was called to be the first assistant in the priests quorum of my student branch. A few months later, after I'd become very active in my branch, I thought back to my decision and wondered how it might have been if I hadn't been baptized before coming to college. Life away from my home, my friends, and my missionaries was very different from my life back home. As things were, I was able to grow in the Church because I was immediately involved in my branch.

But if I had gone to school as a nonmember I wouldn't have had those same opportunities, nor would I have had the same strong LDS friends that I met at church. If I hadn't been a member I would have made my friends among nonmembers, and I'm sure the fragile new testimony I had gained from the missionary discussions would have faded rapidly.

And now, many years later, I still know that was the right decision. I also know that if I need to know the Lord's will regarding any important issue, I can find it through prayer.

Quick and Powerful

R. SCOTT SIMMONS

I believe the Book of Mormon is quick and powerful. Let me share an example of that. In college all of my roommates were former mission companions until one of them got married, and a young man whom we didn't know moved in. We found out later that he was nineteen, and if I remember right, he had actually moved because he was under a lot of pressure from everybody at his former residence to go on a mission. In fact, the first time we met face-to-face I introduced myself, and he said, "Are you going to tell me to go on a mission, too?" I remember thinking, *No, because you'd just be wasting your time and the Lord's with an attitude like that!* I couldn't believe him.

Well, I was concerned about him, and I began to pray to ask Heavenly Father what I could do to help him. It turned out that he and I ate breakfast together every morning because we went to work at the same time. My habit is to read my Book of Mormon while eating my Captain Crunch and Golden Grahams. (I mix the two cereals together because the sugar content is just what I need to get going in the morning.) One morning I was sitting there reading my Book of Mormon and thinking about my roommate and how I might help him, when the thought came to me—and of course it was the Spirit—*Read your Book of Mormon out loud.* I wanted to reply, "Spirit, no, he'll think I'm crazy!"

Can you imagine sitting at the table when someone suddenly just starts reading the Book of Mormon out loud? I didn't know what to do, and I guess I lacked the faith, so instead of reading my Book of Mormon out loud I just looked at my roommate and said, "Ugh, I can't believe this! I just cannot believe these Lamanites!"

And that was it. I just kept reading. I happened to be in the war chapters in Alma, and so the next morning while he was eating his cereal and I was reading my Book of Mormon, I said, "Oh, man! These Lamanites are so dumb! Listen to this . . ." and I read a verse and asked, "Aren't they dumb?"

You're dumb, I'm sure he was thinking. He didn't say that, but I'm sure that's what he thought as he looked at me. I didn't really know quite what I was doing, but I was just trying to follow the promptings of the Spirit. Well, this went on for several weeks, and each morning I would try to do just a little bit more. I would sometimes say to him, "Look, read this!" Then I would hand him my Book of Mormon and ask, "Can you believe it?" I would then continue reading. I wouldn't explain or elaborate; breakfast would just go on. After about two weeks of this, he said to me one morning, "You know, I have one of those books."

"Cool," I said. "Would you like to read with me?"

"Would that be okay?" he asked and ran back to his room and grabbed his Book of Mormon and brought it out and set it down.

From that point on we read together almost every morning throughout the rest of the semester. He then went home for spring break, and all my other roommates moved out. After the break, he came back and became my immediate roommate. Upon his return he said, "Hey, what are you doing this Sunday?" And I said, "Oh, I don't know. I was thinking maybe a little church, ya know, cookies, fireside later, I don't know, it just depends. Why?"

"Well," he said, "they're going to set me apart as an elder today, and I just wondered if you would be there."

I said—and this is just typical of my nature—"Well, how come they're gonna make you an elder?"

"Well," he said, "when I was home I got my papers together and I'm going to serve a mission."

And so I watched him be ordained an elder, and I watched him prepare to serve and fulfill a wonderful mission.

The scriptures are indeed quick and powerful.

A Change of Heart
of

$\mathscr{B}$roken Arms, Broken Hearts, and Confession

BRAD WILCOX

"Everybody make a human pyramid," I called out. It was a large youth gathering. I was helping with some mingling activities and games. "Come on," I cheered. "You can do it."

The groups quickly started piling up. Those on bottom rows pretended not to be in pain. The young people were involved, enthusiastic, and perhaps a little too competitive.

One young man, seeing that his group was falling behind, decided that the best way he could help them was to slow down the group next door. He playfully ran up to the almost completed pyramid and kicked the arm of the boy on the end of the bottom row. Science textbooks say that gravity is a law. Suddenly, twelve teenage bodies obeyed the law and came crashing down on top of one teenage arm.

With no time to lose, I packed the poor victim into my car and rushed him to the hospital, where doctors examined him. The young man listened bravely as they explained everything they would have to do to fix his broken arm. The hospital was busy. The process was drawn out. We went from admitting room to X-ray room to casting room to examination room, waiting in each place as though we were in line for the main attraction at Disneyland.

I felt sorry for my young friend. He had planned to spend his evening at a dance. He had anticipated a night of food, females, and fun. Instead he spent the whole time alone in a hospital with Brother Wilcox.

"So, how many in your family?" I tried to get a conversation started. Along with family, I asked him about his interests and mission plans. We spoke of seminary, sports, school, Scouts, and scriptures. We shared our favorite foods, books, hobbies, and finally, gospel principles. "I think one of my favorites is repentance," I said. "I'm so thankful Christ has given us the chance to change our lives and be better."

Suddenly, my friend became quiet.

In a movie script, this would have been a great time for the doctor to enter. But this wasn't a movie. No doctor came. Finally my friend spoke. "Brother Wilcox, what if someone has done something in the past that he's not really . . ." He paused. "Well, I know you're going to say go see the bishop, but that's the problem. I really can't go talk to him, because he thinks I'm such a good kid, and I don't know how telling him this stuff can help anyway. I would rather that no one ever knew about it."

I had come to the hospital with a young man in urgent need of attention for a broken arm. Now I realized there was a broken heart that needed attention as well. I tried to grasp the teaching moment and asked: "What should someone do if he breaks an arm? Now, I know you're going to say that he should go to the hospital and see the doctor, but that's the problem. The doctor might think he hurt himself. And I don't know how telling a doctor can help a broken arm anyway. Maybe the guy should just go around with his arm broken in five places, feeling severe pain, and not tell anyone."

"Okay, I get the point," my friend admitted. "But I really don't even know where to start."

During the rest of the evening, in between X rays and casts, we talked about the what, who, when, where, why, and how of confession.

When we were finished at the hospital, I escorted my friend, complete with his new white cast, to the car. I said, "It's been a long night for you—in more ways than one." He nodded in agreement. "I challenge you to go see your bishop," I continued.

"He works for God, and you can't get a better physician than that." We hugged—carefully—and I drove him home.

Not long afterwards a letter came: "Dear Brad: How are you? Myself? I am great, fantastic, stupendous, and better and cleaner than I have been since my baptism and it feels sooooo good. I saw my bishop and it was not as bad as I thought it would be. He told me he was glad that I made this decision in my life and that my life would run smoother now. . . . I asked him when I would be forgiven and he assured me that I would know. This week I lived my week normally, riding my bike every day and just hanging around with my friends, but today . . . I was in my room, listening to some Church music, and the Spirit told me I was forgiven and that Jesus really loves me and knows me. It happened so fast that I did not know what was happening until I realized I was bawling like a baby. This is exactly what you said would happen . . . and it is one of the best things that has ever happened to me."

$\mathscr{T}$he Prodigal Daughter

CARLOS E. ASAY

Linda was a very popular seventeen-year-old who loved the noise of the crowd. She seemed happiest when involved in activities where people mingled freely and engaged in boisterous conversation. No one was surprised when she was chosen as a school cheerleader. After all, she could jump and shout and stir excitement among a group of people as well as anyone.

Slowly, but progressively, the voices of the peer group gained control of Linda's life, for she wanted to be acceptable to everyone, particularly to those who seemed to be the most sophisticated and "fun" oriented. In time the enticements of her carnally minded friends became more appealing than the warnings of her caring parents. Worse still, the numbing effects of tobacco, alcohol, and other addictive substances little by little smothered the voice of conscience. Before long, Linda yielded completely to the voices of the world—voices that had convinced her that happiness could be gained by forsaking parental restraints, rules of society, and other quieting influences in her life.

At the urgings of a lustful companion, Linda ran away from home. They were not concerned about marriage or other conventional arrangements. It was the "good time" that the two sought. Thoughts of basking under the lights of the big city and blending their voices with others who were rebelling against heaven and home seemed to push them on their way.

Once in the city, the young couple chased their dismal dream. It was one binge after another and one nightclub after another, with all the assorted baggage attached. Soon, however, the dream turned into a nightmare. Their funds were exhausted. Too proud and ashamed to return home, they looked for jobs and some means of sustaining their style of living in the so-called "fast lane." But it wasn't easy for two high school dropouts to find employment. Neither possessed a marketable skill, and what friends they had made during the short and carefree days pushed them aside.

As their circumstances became more desperate, Linda and her companion began to blame each other for what had happened. Eventually they decided to go it alone, because the stresses of adversity had destroyed all that remained of their pseudo-love.

Linda moved from one job to another—one economic crisis to another. First, it was washing dishes in a dirty café. Next, it was sweeping the floor in a smelly saloon. Each task was more demeaning than the last and each took its toll on her ego and self-esteem. Finally, in sheer desperation, Linda turned to prostitution.

A year passed, but it seemed like an eternity to Linda. Her life was one one-night stand after another with a parade of nameless individuals who treated her like a rented tool. She became zombie-like, hardly heeding the meaningless voices around her and the bright lights of the big city—lights that had drawn her away from home and burned her like an innocent moth. Life, she finally concluded, was not worth living.

One evening, Linda decided that things must change. She crawled out of bed without awakening her bed partner, dressed, and walked the noisy streets of the city. She wondered what she might do to escape her dreary and empty existence.

In the midst of Linda's aimless wandering, thoughts of home flooded through her mind. She remembered the warmth and beauty of the place where Mother and Father showered her with love. She recalled many fond memories associated with brothers, sisters, and other members of the family circle. Moreover, she brooded over the feelings of peace and security that had once been hers when living within the quiet company of people who had extended unselfish love to her. Her heart yearned for home and the voice within cried, "Go there!"

But she had concerns. She wondered whether those at home would accept her after all the mistakes she had made. Will they forgive me? was the question that repeated itself over and over again in her mind.

Then she remembered a lesson her father had taught the family about the forgiveness of sins after repentance and through the merits of Christ. Moreover, she recalled her father reading and discussing the parable of the prodigal son—a tender story that had caused her and other listeners to weep openly.

Linda thought to herself: I am the prodigal; I did rebel; I have erred; and I have eaten with the swine. So I must go home and trust that they will receive me.

She had barely enough money to buy a one-way bus ticket home; yet she bought it, knowing of no other way to climb out of the pit she had dug for herself. It was a long ride back to the little town where she had grown up. The miles seemed to drag by. En route she replayed the twelve-month nightmare over and over again in her mind. How foolish she had been! Why had she listened to the enticing voices of the world? With each thought came regrets and bitter tears.

The walk from the bus station to home seemed long and arduous. Part of Linda's body wanted to run. Another part held back because of the uncertainties of the reception. One voice within her shouted, "Turn back, they don't want to see you ever again." A still, small voice whispered, "They love you and they want you to come back home."

She hesitated in front of the house. But as she reached to open the front gate to the yard, the door of the house flew open and out streamed the whole family. All members of the family cradled her in their arms and smothered her with kisses, for this their daughter and sister "was dead and is alive again; and was lost, and is found" (Luke 15:32).

Later in the day Linda learned of the power that turned her homeward. She was informed that family and friends had gathered on that weekend fasting and praying that she would be found and returned safely to their care. The loud and barbaric voices of Blindness of Mind and Hardness of Heart had lured her away from loved ones. Soft and kind voices—even the enticings of the Holy Spirit—had brought her back.

It is important that you keep in mind the miracle of forgiveness through the goodness and grace of our Savior. Many rejoice when the sinner comes to himself and repents. But it is also very important that you remember this unchanging truth: "That man [or woman] who resists temptation and lives without sin is far better off than the man [or woman] who has fallen, no matter how repentant the latter may be. . . . How much better it is never to have committed the sin!" (Spencer W. Kimball, *The Miracle of Forgiveness* [Salt Lake City: Bookcraft, 1969], p. 357).

*G*rizzly

JACK R. CHRISTIANSON

C hristmas Eve 1988 was bitter cold. The thermometer had plunged below zero, and eighteen to twenty-four inches of snow blanketed the ground. It was a day when wise people were inside with the heater turned up, the fire blazing, and a blanket wrapped securely around them.

My family was busy preparing for our customary Christmas Eve activities: meeting in our family room to open one gift apiece, eating great food, and witnessing the yearly reenactment of the Christmas story found in the second chapter of Luke in the New Testament.

The smell of cooking turkey and pumpkin pie filled the house with savory aromas. I guess. I couldn't smell them. My nose felt stuffy, my head pounded, my entire body ached with the flu. Everyone was having a marvelous time. Everyone but me. Staying in bed, sick, on Christmas Eve is not my idea of fun. However, I knew if I didn't I wouldn't be well enough to enjoy Christmas morning.

I tried to give orders from bed, but no one seemed to pay much attention, especially when I asked my daughters to let out our dog, Grizzly, for a few minutes.

No one moved. They weren't going outside for anyone. My three oldest daughters all had "reasons" why none of them could go. Finally, however, Rebecca (the oldest daughter) let Grizzly out through the front door. But she didn't stay with him, being driven inside by the cold.

A couple of hours later I asked if anyone had let the dog out. Silence was all that came up the stairs into my bedroom. Then

Rebecca's anxious voice pierced the quiet. "Oh, Dad, I'm sorry! I forgot about the dog!"

I leaped from my bed, dressed quickly, and ran outside. My illness seemed to remain in the bedroom. It was replaced by the fear of losing my prized golden retriever.

Yelling and whistling for the dog proved fruitless. When the dog did not respond I knew one of two things had happened: either he had been hit by a car or he had been stolen. He had always come before when called.

My heart was sick. My wife, Melanie, and I split up to search for him through the biting cold. We met a few minutes later at the corner, both frozen and wanting the warmth and comfort of our home.

While we discussed our next plan of action, a man pulled up in a blue van.

"Are you Jack Christianson?" he asked calmly.

"Yes, sir. Who are you?"

He told me his name and continued, with some hesitation, "I'm your paperboy's father. Your dog followed my son home from his paper route and was hit by a truck in front of our home. Would you please come and decide what you want to do with the body?"

"Is he dead?" I asked, with little hope in my voice.

"Not yet," he replied sadly. "But I'm not sure how long he'll stay alive."

We climbed into the van in silence. Quietly we rode to the scene of the accident. Melanie didn't say anything but covered her face with her hands in order to camouflage her tears. It didn't work. The tears dripped off the heels of her hands into her lap.

Our eyes met. Through her eyes, she communicated a heart-felt message. "I'm sorry, Jack. I know how much you love your dog."

When we arrived at the scene of the accident, a crowd of concerned neighbors stood around the dog's broken body, now covered with someone's coat.

One of the neighbors was coming with a blanket as we approached the dog, and the animal-control officer had already arrived with an ambulance. Okay, it wasn't really an ambulance; it was an animal-control truck with a cage in the back. But I viewed it as the ambulance that would transport Grizzly to the hospital for treatment.

The sound of my voice brought Grizzly's head up off the cement. His body was stretched across the curb, the front half lying on the sidewalk and the hind legs lying helplessly in the gutter.

He tried to get up, but his efforts were in vain. Both back legs were shattered. I calmed him by speaking in soft tones and giving love pats on his head and neck. I cried as I checked out his condition.

When I checked his eyes and gums, it was obvious he was quickly going into shock. I asked the officer if there was a veterinarian on call somewhere in the vicinity.

"It's Christmas Eve," he said, somewhat hesitantly. "But I'll try anyway."

While he talked with the dispatcher, an older gentleman bundled up in a winter parka and a dirty baseball cap approached us slowly.

"That your dog, son?" he asked, trying to fight back tears.

"Yeah."

"There was nothing I could do! He just darted in front of my truck! I didn't even have time to hit my brakes."

"It's okay," I said. "I'm sure there was nothing you could have done."

"I'm sorry, son. I'm sorry."

I felt as sorry for him as I did for the dog. He walked away, dejected, hands in his pockets, his head down, mumbling through tears how sorry he was.

"I found one!" the officer said. "The vet will meet us at his office in fifteen to twenty minutes. He's at the mall finishing his Christmas shopping, but he said your golden retriever was worth stopping everything else."

"Thanks," I muttered as I picked up my friend Grizzly and walked toward the "ambulance."

The man who had brought us to the scene of the accident gave my wife a ride home, while the officer and I transported my dog to the "hospital."

Melanie arrived at the veterinarian's office shortly after I had carried Grizzly in and placed him on a long coal-black table. As she watched the doctor and me work on Grizzly, she covered her face with her hands, again trying to hide her tears. It didn't work. Again they found their way to the heels of her hands and then onto the black-and-white-checkered tile floor. She was as heartbroken for me as she was for the dog.

Approximately two and a half hours later the doctor gave me the bad news.

"I'm sorry, Jack. I've done all I can do, short of surgery, and I don't think Griz will live through that. It would cost a few hundred dollars, and he'd never make it," he said sadly. "My suggestion is that we put him to sleep. Would you like some time to think about it and to talk it over with your wife?" he asked sympathetically.

"Sure. Thanks," I said, trying now to fight back my tears.

Melanie and I decided it would be best to let Grizzly's suffering end. So, after a few minutes alone with my faithful friend, I kissed him good-bye, asked him to forgive me, and then asked the doctor to do his part quickly.

Within ten seconds after the doctor injected a drug into Grizzly's right front leg, the dog's eyes rolled upward and he was dead. I cried.

Later, while making arrangements for Grizzly's burial, I asked the doctor what he did with the bodies of deceased animals. He said he usually sent them to California. A truck would come for pickup on the following Tuesday, and the weather was cold enough that Grizzly's body would stay frozen until then. I then asked what happened when the bodies reached California. I was sickened at the response.

"Oh, they make fertilizer or glue out of them," he said, without batting an eye.

My mind quickly thought about all the white paste or glue I had eaten out of those big white jars in elementary school. My stomach turned at the thought.

I instantly determined that my favorite dog was not going to be used as paste in some elementary school somewhere, ending up on the back side of a picture of Abraham Lincoln or George Washington. I made arrangements to take Grizzly and bury him myself.

How would I tell the children that our dear friend was gone? They would be heartbroken. When I told them, they asked if they could kiss him good-bye before we laid him to rest. I know some people would think it was morbid for sweet young girls to kiss a dead, stiff dog, but he was part of our family.

My father arrived later to help with the burial. We put the chains on my car tires and drove to the foothills of Mount Timpanogos, overlooking Utah Valley. He had recently returned from a mission, so we had much to talk about as we fought the frozen ground and rocky soil while digging the grave.

As I continued to pick away at the earth, thoughts of pioneer mothers leaving their dead children in shallow graves all along the westward trail plagued my mind. I was only burying a dog. How would it feel to lay a child or spouse to rest under a thin blanket of snow, or wrapped in a quilt and placed under a bush? Tears found their way off the end of my nose or to the back of my hand as I tried to hide them from my dad. Feelings were deep. A new and deeper appreciation for ancestors was being born. How did they endure?

With these thoughts burning in my mind, I helped lift a large rock in place as a headstone. We had finished our painful task.

We rested, leaning on the handles of our shovel and pick. The sun's long white rays filtered through some evening clouds and rested upon Utah Lake. It was beautiful and peaceful, but bitter cold.

The silence was broken when I asked my dad a question, and the ensuing conversation proved to have a profound influence in my life.

"Can you believe I feel this way over a silly dog?"

"No!" he said quickly. "You've lost countless dogs and other animals, son. Why would this one be so different?"

I don't remember answering specifically. But I do remember asking him another question. Little thought went into it at that moment, but it began a process of profound thought and led to a rich, religious experience between a father and his grown son.

"Dad, if you and I, as mortals, can weep at the loss of a dog, how must a God in heaven feel when he loses one of his children?"

"What?" he questioned.

"Think about it. If we, as mortals, with all of our frailties and imperfections, can weep when we lose a pet; cannot God, the Almighty, the perfect one, weep when his children choose to abandon him or seek not to return to his presence?"

There on the hillside overlooking the valley where my dad had raised me, a father and son had a deep religious experience discussing the worth of souls in the sight of God. It was too cold to talk long, but seeds were planted deeply, not to be forgotten with the melting snow.

Two or three days after Grizzly's death I tried to find another puppy to take his place. I contacted the people who had sold him to me. They offered to give us his mother if we would breed her with a particular male and then give them a puppy. After looking at the mother dog, Ginger, I decided to do it. She was the same color as Grizzly, but two or three inches shorter at the shoulder, and her neck and head were not as large. Otherwise she looked just like Grizzly. I brought her home and provided a place for her in the garage.

A few months later my daughters helped me deliver nine golden retriever puppies in that same garage. As the puppies were born, I couldn't help but ask the question: "Girls, if you and I can get so excited over the birth of puppies, cannot God in heaven rejoice when we accept him and are born again?" I then quoted Doctrine and Covenants 18:13, "And how great is his joy in the soul that repenteth!"

They thought it was an odd way to teach a lesson, but I hope they felt something positive.

"*I* Just Can't Pray"

R. SCOTT SIMMONS

As a seminary teacher I once invited my classes to pray morning and night for an entire week, and then at the end of the week we had a testimony meeting on prayer where my students shared their experiences. Everyone in each of my classes shared something with us except for one young woman—one young woman who I never would have expected not to pray. And so after class I caught her and said, "Hey, what happened? What's up? Why didn't you pray?" And she replied, "Oh, Brother Simmons, I just can't. I just can't pray." I challenged her to try again. And she said, "I will." But when she came back and I asked her about it, she sadly answered that she hadn't been able to.

So we stepped into my office. And I said, "You have got to tell me what in the world could be so serious that you couldn't pray." And then it came out. She didn't tell me any specifics, because I asked her not to and because that's not my place. She had done some things that had caused her to feel unworthy, like she couldn't approach her Father in Heaven in prayer. Well, immediately I had her turn to 2 Nephi 32. Verse 8 says: "And now, my beloved brethren, I perceive that ye ponder still in your hearts; and it grieveth me that I must speak concerning this thing. For if ye would hearken unto the Spirit which teacheth a man to pray ye would know ye must pray; for the evil spirit teacheth not a man to pray, but teacheth him that he must not pray."

So, if you ever feel that you can't pray, where does that feeling come from? It comes from the adversary. Your Father in Heaven would never, under any circumstances, want you to not pray to Him; but the adversary would. The adversary doesn't want you to have the experiences that come with prayer. He doesn't want you to feel God's love, because he knows that when you do, the Spirit will invite you to change.

I continued talking to this young lady by reading verse 9: "But behold, I say unto you that ye must pray always, and not faint." In old English the word *faint* essentially means to "give up." So we need to pray always and not give up.

And so I said to her, "I'll tell you what, let's you and I pray right now. I'll offer a prayer and then you offer one. How does that sound?"

"Okay," she said. And so we knelt down, and I prayed a really simple prayer: "Heavenly Father, help her to know how much she's loved." And then I said to her, "Okay, go." And she said, "My dear Heavenly Father," and then she just started to sob. And finally she said, "In the name of Jesus Christ, amen." That was her whole prayer. But when she stood up, all she could say to me over and over again was, "Brother Simmons, He still loves me. He still loves me."

$\mathcal{M}$arissa's Choice

ELAINE CANNON

When I was the youth editor for the *Deseret News* I spent a lot of time listening to troubled teenagers. Marissa was one of them. She had lived for a time in a big city with a large university at its hub. She had dropped out of school after the first quarter and worked in the food services to earn money for the next round. She was the salad-and-steak-bar girl who catered to athletes. She was pretty and feminine, with a personality to match. Naturally the school's athletic heroes were attracted to her. They dished up their male charm while she dished up mixed greens. It was a losing game for Marissa, because the flirting that started out in fun ultimately ended up in childbirth.

Marriage was not an option, so the first major decision was whether to allow the pregnancy to go forward. Marissa opted to reject abortion. When she came back home to have the baby, we spent a lot of time counseling together.

The second, and maybe the toughest, decision was made after hours of talking matters over, together with her parents. Should she keep the baby or give it up? She decided to give up the baby for adoption.

The final decision was choosing the adoptive parents. Marissa wanted to have some say in this, even though she wouldn't actually know the names of the adoptive families being considered.

We agreed about the likelihood that Heavenly Father would be interested in where that spirit child of his would be placed. This has been my experience with countless cases of unwed mothers and illegitimate babies.

(Time out for an opinion: I use the term *illegitimate* even though the world has largely abandoned it. I believe we should tell it like it is. We should remind young people who offend-in-love that fooling around out of wedlock can bring into the world babies that are outside legal family status. Illegitimate. This is too high a price to pay—for the child, the unwed mother, responsible grandparents, and for other youth who see the poor example. One day, more of the culpable boys may start suffering too when they understand more clearly their own part in such a situation.)

Marissa did a lot of praying during that period of time. A month or so later she came back to see me. She brought with her pictures of her baby taken at birth and a copy of the letter she had written to leave with the adoptive mother until the appropriate day for the child to receive it in later years.

Then she shared special feelings with me about the whole heartbreaking experience. She was glad she had prayed a lot about where that baby was placed. It kept her close to Heavenly Father. It led her to true repentance and an unselfish desire to do what was right for this newborn. She was thankful that she had asked for a bishop's blessing as she went into labor. Her mother had asked for one, too, that she might support her daughter in the decision to give the child for adoption.

"I gave up my life, for her," explained Marissa. "At least I gave her up so that she could have the best possible chance. Some people feel as if they own their offspring. But after talking with you I came to really understand that she wasn't my baby at all, ever. I made a mistake and I paid a price for it. But that's no reason for the baby to suffer.

"You know, I finally felt forgiven. The Spirit flooded over me when I made a firm decision about the adoptive family and I carefully signed the papers. I felt akin to the Savior, who gave up his life for us. I sacrificed for the baby that she might have a good life. I have no regrets or adjustments now, you see. I didn't 'give up' my baby. I took every prayerful precaution I could to make a blessing out of a mess. I wasn't a bad girl, you see," she explained. "I was a good girl gone wrong, and I had to make up for it."

Actually, when questioned later, Marissa admitted it would have been a good idea for her to have prayed as hard for her own life as she did for her baby's—and to have done so earlier. Maybe then she wouldn't have suffered this heartache at all.

$\mathcal{O}$f Foolish Ventures

WAYNE B. LYNN

$\mathcal{S}$omething was wrong with my dog, Spotty. I could tell by the way he was acting. Without his usual bounding, barking, tail-wagging greeting, he slipped quietly like a shadow around the corner of the building.

Sensing his need for my attention, I, too, slipped around the building to learn the reason for his strange behavior. A quick glance told the story. Spotty's face was bristling with white pointed slivers that gave him the look of a grizzled old prospector with a face covered with whiskers. He whimpered pleadingly, rubbed his nose toward the ground, and pawed at his face and lips trying to remove the cause of his pain. A porcupine had driven a multitude of sharp quills deep into his tender nose and quivering flesh.

He saw me now and looked up toward me with pleading eyes as if to say, "I know I have been foolish. I should have known better, but won't you please help me?" He made another futile pass at the cruel barbs protruding from his bloodied face, which merely added to his pain and further proved the hopelessness of his situation.

I walked over to my nearby car, removed a pair of pliers from the glove compartment, and walked back toward him. "This is going to hurt, old fella," I said softly as I carefully pillowed his pain-ridden head in my lap. He looked back at me with limpid eyes as if to say, "I understand."

As I began the painful extractions, I talked to him quietly. I suppose I was talking to myself as much as I was to him. "What would you do without me now, old fella? You are in a rather hopeless situation, aren't you? How would you ever get these quills out by yourself?" He looked directly at me, and I felt he understood. I wondered what would have happened to him if I had not come to his aid. I could imagine those painful barbs finding their way deeper and deeper into fevered flesh. In my mind I could see his face festering and swelling as the pain became so unrelenting that old Spotty would do almost anything to escape from it.

How like old Spotty we are, I thought to myself. *How many times do we find ourselves in foolish circumstances from which we cannot escape?*

My thoughts carried me to a man kneeling in a garden alone. Upon him was placed the burden of all the sins of the world. The weight of this debt brought pain and anguish beyond our understanding—pain of such magnitude that he, the Son of God, sweat blood from every pore. I thought of my own life, of foolish ventures that brought me sorrow; but because of this man kneeling alone in the garden, I could be spared. Jesus had done for me that which I could not do for myself. My pain could be removed, my tortured spirit healed. I could look up once again with hope and promise.

I could feel old Spotty tremble with pain each time I touched him, but he made no protest. Finally, the last quill was removed from his sad face. I stroked his fevered head gently and felt the warm softness of his fur beneath my fingertips. With painful effort he lifted his head and turned with gratitude to lick my hand.

My thought returned to Jesus long ago. His feet were bathed in tears and dried with the hair of a repentant sinner. I longed to show my love to him, to bathe his feet with my tears, to kneel before him and show my love.

Spotty was all right now. He rose stiffly and walked cautiously away with his tail inscribing small arcs of happiness. We had learned something today, Spotty and I—something for which I am grateful.

The Poison of an Unforgiving Spirit

H. BURKE PETERSON

For much of our lives my family and I lived in central Arizona. Some years ago a group of teenagers from our local high school went on an all-day picnic into the desert on the outskirts of Phoenix. As some of you know, the desert foliage is rather sparse—mostly mesquite, catclaw, and paloverde trees, with a few cactus scattered here and there. In the heat of the summer, where there are thickets of this desert growth, you may also find rattlesnakes as unwelcome residents. These young people were picnicking and playing, and during their frolicking one of the girls was bitten on the ankle by a rattlesnake. As is the case with such a bite, the rattler's fangs released venom almost immediately into her bloodstream.

This very moment was a time for critical decision. They could immediately begin to extract the poison from her leg, or they could search out the snake and destroy it. Their decision made, the girl and her young friends pursued the snake. It slipped quickly into the undergrowth and avoided them for fifteen or twenty minutes. Finally they found it, and rocks and stones soon avenged the infliction.

Then they remembered: their companion had been bitten! They became aware of her discomfort, as by now the venom had had time to move from the surface of the skin deep into the tissues of her foot and leg. Within another thirty minutes they were at the emergency room of the hospital. By then, the venom was well into its work of destruction.

A couple of days later I was informed of the incident and was asked by some young members of the Church to visit their friend in the hospital. As I entered her room, I saw a pathetic sight. Her foot and leg were elevated and were swollen almost beyond recognition. The tissue in her limb had been destroyed by the poison, and a few days later it was found that her leg would have to be amputated below the knee.

It was a senseless sacrifice, this price of revenge. How much better it would have been if, after the young woman had been bitten, there had been an extraction of the venom from the leg in a process known to all desert dwellers.

There are those today who have been bitten—or offended, if you will—by others. What can be done? What will you do when hurt by another? The safe way, the sure way, the right way is to look inward and immediately start the cleansing process. The wise and the happy person removes first the impurities from within. The longer the poison of resentment and unforgiveness stays in a body, the greater and longer lasting is its destructive effect. The poison of revenge, or of unforgiving thoughts or attitudes, unless removed, will destroy the soul in which it is harbored.

The Lord has said, "For if ye forgive men their trespasses, your heavenly Father will also forgive you: but if ye forgive not men their trespasses, neither will your Father forgive your trespasses" (Matthew 6:14–15).

And he further added, "For he that forgiveth not his brother his trespasses standeth condemned before the Lord; for there remaineth in him the greater sin" (D&C 64:9).

Let us dismiss from our beings—and purge from our souls—the venom of any feeling of ill will or bitterness toward anyone. Let us strike from our hearts the unwillingness to forgive and forget, and instead approach men in the spirit of the Master, even those who "despitefully use you" (Matthew 5:44). Let us pray—rather, let us plead—for the spirit of forgiveness. Let us look for the good in each other—not the flaws.

Work
and
Goals

From Third to First

SHANE BARKER

The bat cracked as the ball shot toward the outfield fence, and Chris Gates dashed for first base. He hit the bag at top speed and turned toward second.

The center fielder charged after the ball, scooping it out of the grass and rifling it toward second. Chris slid face-first in the dirt, beating the ball by a whisker.

"All right, Chris!" someone shouted. "Way to hit the ball! Good job out there!"

Chris stood up and dusted red dirt from his uniform. He grinned.

Chris played third base on his high school's sophomore baseball team. He was a powerful hitter and was one of the best fielders on the team.

One time, during a game against a rival school, Chris was standing just inside the third-base line when the batter cracked a shot straight toward left field. Chris leaped for the ball like an F-16 going for takeoff. He went straight up, putting his glove into space just as the ball got there. He curled up and hit the ground rolling, but still managed to hang on to the ball.

Another time, a batter sliced a grounder that went smoking through the grass toward third base. As quick as a cat, Chris darted after it. He knew the ball was going to be just out of reach, so he dived for it. But while he was in the air the ball hit something and bounced to the side. Chris had to reach behind him, catching the ball with his bare hand before he smacked into the grass.

It was the most spectacular play I'd ever seen. Or at least it would have been, except for one thing: Chris tried to throw the ball.

Jumping to his feet, he took quick aim and rifled the ball toward first. He overshot the first baseman by about three feet, not only allowing the runner to make base, but letting him reach second, too.

The coach came screaming from the dugout.

"What in the world are you trying to do?" he shouted. "That guy's not seven feet tall! You've got to keep the ball down so that he can at least have a shot at *jumping* for it!"

Now, Chris felt bad enough about his mistake. Making a bad throw had allowed a man on base. And it nearly cost his team the game.

"Fielding's never been a problem for me," he told me. "I'm quick on my feet and I hardly even have to look at the ball. I know where it's going and I just seem to get my glove in the right place at the right time. But throwing . . ." He shook his head. "Well, I'm not really very accurate."

It wasn't that he didn't try. He used to practice all the time. Standing out on the grass behind the school he would practice throwing for hours. But it didn't help. No matter how much he practiced, he couldn't throw the ball in a straight line.

"Everybody tells me I throw like a girl," he said. "But I've never been able to change that. There's something about my arm . . . it just won't rotate the way it's supposed to."

The sad thing is that it was always getting him in trouble with his coaches.

Finally, tired of getting yelled at all the time, Chris tried something different. He went to the coach and asked to play somewhere besides third base.

"I told him that I was the best fielder on the team," he said. "And I told him that I was a good hitter, too. All we needed was to find a place where my throwing wouldn't hurt us so much."

Chris was convincing enough that the coach was willing to give him a chance. So Chris moved from third base to first. There, his spectacular fielding was an asset. And though he occasionally muffed a double play on the throw to second, his poor throwing wasn't a major liability.

Chris was the team MVP that season, and the next year he made the high school varsity team. All because he was able to get his coach to look past his weak point and see his best.

$\mathcal{N}$ot Afraid to Try

WAYNE B. LYNN

I recall a time, from my days as a shop teacher in high school, when my students competed with students from other schools to demonstrate skills acquired in their shop training. One of my regular team members failed to appear, leaving us one man short. I was anxious to find an instant replacement to meet the number required for team competition. A freshman was working nearby on some construction. I had previously noted his willingness to tackle any kind of project. Not by inspiration but out of desperation, I enlisted him for my team and gave him a thirty-minute crash course on how to weld with an oxyacetylene welding torch. To say that he was ill-prepared is an understatement.

Soon we were off to the neighboring town, experiencing the thrill of competition. My little freshman was thrown to the wolves. It was like suiting him up in a football uniform for the first time and then sending him into the thick of a varsity ball game. There was a dramatic contrast between the metal pieces he welded and the ones welded by the senior boy who won the contest. The piece so skillfully welded by the winner was nearly a piece of art. The weld was smooth and strong. It penetrated the metal as a good weld should. He had clearly mastered this useful skill.

My freshman was undaunted, however, by what could have been an embarrassing situation. I watched him congratulate the winner and heard him make a rather startling request: "Can I have your welded piece to take home with me?"

Puzzled by the request, the winner replied, "Of course you can."

It was particularly satisfying for me to watch that boy in the days that followed. Each shop period I watched him working in the corner of the shop where the welders were kept. Wearing goggles and protective gloves, he worked under rising smoke, practicing his welding skills. Next to his own work he always placed the prize-winning weld of his former competitor. When it wasn't out for observation, it was always in his shop coverall pocket. He was determined to make a weld to match that one. His efforts were sustained by such a stubborn determination that it became a joke among some of the other students. Following each shop class he would have a circle around each eye, battle marks from the welder's goggles held tightly around his head by an elastic band.

In the beginning his welds were crude. Instruction, observation, and encouragement helped, but improvement came primarily from his constant practice and determination. You can guess the outcome of this story. One day I thrilled to watch him walk across the stage of a packed auditorium to receive recognition for outstanding acetylene welding in state competition. He not only matched the weld in his pocket, he made a better one. He was not afraid to try. By applying this kind of determination to other goals in his life, he went on to other achievements.

$\mathcal{H}$ow Far Is Forty-nine Yards?

MELVIN LEAVITT

$\mathbf{A}$ detached pom-pom streamer rustles up off the track in a light breeze and then falls; an empty soft drink cup bump, bump, bumps down the bleachers. A cheerleader, seeing that no one is listening, falls silent in the middle of a timid "go team!" An absolute hush and stillness envelops the crowd; the flag hangs limp. Even the crimson and gold leaves of the trees beyond the scoreboard are motionless, and the low sun of a cold autumn afternoon seems to wait. A young man in a green and white jersey leans forward, his arms hanging limp. Then there is the snap, the distant clash of shoulder pads, the steps, the flashing shoe; and as the ball distorts under the impact of the square toe, there is an exhalation of breath, and then a roar from both bleachers while the ball is still in the air—while it's still too early to tell.

There is no man on any football field so alone as the field goal kicker at his moment of truth. Every eye is on him. Every fan is for him or against him, and the work of a moment will leave him the hero or the scapegoat.

The fellow in the green and white jersey is seventeen-year-old Latter-day Saint Brad Cordery. He kicks field goals and PATs (point after touchdown) for the Olympus High School football team in Salt Lake City, Utah.

Brad is a good one. He has a forty-nine yarder under his belt and has converted thirty out of thirty-eight PATs for 70 percent. And most of the PATs he failed to convert involved bad snaps or blocked kicks.

It doesn't seem very pertinent to him, and most fans don't even know it, but Brad kicks with an artificial leg. He was born with a deformed right foot and stunted lower leg, so his foot was amputated when he was still a baby to make it possible for him to wear an artificial limb. But as opponents who let the Olympus team inside the thirty-yard line can testify, it's no handicap when it comes to kicking field goals.

It hasn't stopped Brad from doing much else either. He says: "A handicap is in the mind first. I could tell myself, 'I have an artificial leg; something's wrong with me.' I could really feel bad and go into my room and lock myself up or something, but what good would that do?

"I don't feel I have a handicap," he insists. "I think I've overcome it, and it's no problem anymore. The handicap is in other people who don't understand. It's no handicap to me."

Brad's preoccupation with goals isn't confined to the football field either. At a young age he learned to meet challenges, mastering his artificial limb so well that he could hold his own in sports competition with his young friends, and it became an unwritten goal to live a completely normal life. It is a goal that he has entirely realized. His experience with the Aaronic Priesthood Personal Achievement Program converted him to the importance of writing down his goals, and goal achievement became a guiding principle in his life.

When Brad set a goal, it had a way of getting accomplished. He decided to become an Eagle Scout with three palms; and he did it. He decided to meet his Aaronic Priesthood Personal Achievement goals, earn his Duty to God award, maintain a high GPA in school, and become a place kicker and kick a forty-yard field goal; and he did them all. He decided to become proficient in basketball, volleyball, softball, handball, tennis, swimming, karate, and golf (among others); and he did it. He decided to learn to both snow and water ski; and he did it.

Brad feels that goals are essential. "If you don't have some definite goals and keep them in front of you, I don't see how you can accomplish very much in life," he says. He also adds a more practical note, however. "You can write goals down," he says. "You can see them; you can think about them; but all your thinking won't do any good unless you decide what you're going to do to accomplish them and then do it."

Brad's approach to football illustrates this attitude. The summer before his sophomore year he had the man who makes his artificial legs throw together a makeshift kicking leg out of a wooden block on the end of an old "fishing leg," a sort of plastic peg leg that Brad uses for swimming and showering. He then hit the practice field with an armful of footballs, his family, and half the neighborhood kids to help retrieve balls. Then he kicked and kicked and kicked and kicked, and when the kids had become tired of it and had gone home, he kicked some more while his father held for him. He kicked, and learned to allow for wind, and kicked, and got his timing down, and kicked some more. Even with the ad-libbed leg, his aim was deadly.

That fall, with a brand-new, made-to-order kicking leg, he was suited up and kicking field goals and PATs for the sophomore team. As a junior, he was the starting place kicker for both the varsity and junior varsity teams.

"He's a real competitor," his football coach says. "He's always emotionally ready to play. He's a hard worker, and he has a good positive attitude. Those things are important for any position."

Brad's entry into the football scene wasn't an easy one. He had to miss several games his sophomore year because of a rule dispute about artificial limbs, and he had to earn his assignment in the face of some talented competition.

"The kids on the team don't look at Brad as someone who's handicapped; they just think of him as a valuable player," his coach emphasizes. "He's the best kicker on the team. He had to compete with another very fine kicker for the position, and Brad just plain beat him out. He's the best kicker I've had in my years of coaching. I've always made it clear to Brad that he's got to make the team on his own. He's not going to play just because he's handicapped. He's got to be the best, and he *is* the best."

Once a year most of us get out a clean sheet of paper and write down a list of New Year's resolutions we have absolutely no intention of keeping. We find plenty of "handicaps" along the way to use as excuses for failure, and then next year we still have the same unaccomplished goals to put down on another clean sheet of paper.

This year when we get ready to abandon the last resolution on the list, perhaps we should form a mental picture of a red-headed young man with freckles, in a green and white jersey, with absolutely no handicaps, lining up a field goal.

Maybe we can't all kick a forty-nine-yard field goal; our talents don't all lie in the same areas. But we can do a lot more than we are doing, and there's no better time to begin than right now.

That's part of Brad's philosophy too. "What you do now—your habits, studies, morals, goals—it all adds up to what you're going to be in the end."

Editor's Note: The preceding selection is part of a longer story that was originally published in 1974. Much has happened in Brad Cordery's life since that time. After high school he served a mission in Arcadia, California, then went on to college and earned a bachelor's degree in community health education and a master's degree in social work. Employed for seventeen years working for LDS Social Services' therapeutic day treatment program, he now works for Salt Lake City. He also is a real estate investor and is involved with financial services. In the Church he has served as a bishop and as a high councilor, and at this writing he is an assistant Scoutmaster in a special needs Mutual program. He and his wife, Marilee, are the parents of four children, and the family resides in West Jordan, Utah.

$\mathscr{A}$ Beet Field Lesson

CARLOS E. ASAY

Early one Saturday morning, my father came to my bedroom and asked if I would be willing to work that day on the Church welfare farm. The assignment was to thin beets in the company of other volunteer laborers from our rural community. Though I had other things planned for that day, I agreed to help, providing the job would be completed by noon.

I was an expert at this slave-like labor—a labor that required a person to walk in a stooped position up and down rows of sugar beets, chopping with a small hoe in one hand and pulling excess plants with the other. It was a tedious task requiring more brawn than brain and more endurance than expertise. However, I could do nearly an acre in one day if I started before sunup, ended long after sundown, and cared little about the pain of standing erect afterwards.

One of the older workers at the farm on that occasion was my stake president, a banker by profession. He was a businessman not accustomed to manual labor. In all honesty, it pleased me to see him digging in the soil and sweating under the hot sun, for this was the first time I had seen this very proper and fastidious Church leader dressed in anything other than a dark suit, white shirt, and conservative tie. And I must admit that I enjoyed watching him get dirt on his hands and clothes. (I was so carried away by this pleasure [heaven forgive me!] that I sped up the soiling process by deliberately kicking up clouds of dust in his direction whenever I worked by his side.)

When the task was nearly completed, President H. Roland Tietjen invited me to speak with him. I stopped my work, laid down my hoe, and sat upon the soft ground beside the kindly man who was one of the most respected citizens in the town.

He asked, "Carlos, how old are you?"

"Eighteen," I replied.

"Do you know how old I am?" he continued.

"Oh, about seventy," was my quick and foolish answer. (I missed the mark by several years.)

Laughing without and, I supposed, crying within, he said, "My time on earth is running out; yours is just beginning. Carlos, would you sell to me the next ten years of your life?"

I thought to myself, What is wrong with President Tietjen? Can't he forget buying and selling for just one morning?

He was able to discern my thoughts and to sense my discomfort with the improbable proposition placed before me. Said he: "I know it is impossible for you to transfer part of your life to me. But if it were possible, would you sell?"

"No!" I blurted out with little thought or reflection. "I would not sell to you or anyone else."

"Suppose I offered you a hundred thousand dollars for these ten years," he pressed. (This was before the day of double- and triple-digit inflation.)

Again I declined his offer, asserting that I had things to do in the years ahead and that I would not sell a part of my life for any amount of money.

During the ten years that followed the beet field conversation, my visits with President Tietjen were few and scattered. Yet, whenever we met, he would refer back to the original question and ask, "Will you accept ninety thousand dollars for the remaining nine years? Eighty thousand for the next eight?" And so it went until the ten years had come and gone.

It did not require a full decade for me to appreciate the profound lesson my wonderful and caring Church leader had taught. I knew he loved me and wanted me to make the most of my life. I knew he wanted me to treasure those formative years between eighteen and twenty-eight—a time when important decisions of eternal consequence are made. Moreover, I knew he wanted to motivate me to set goals, make plans, and initiate actions that would enable me to make the most of my future opportunities.

The Most Important Goal

MICHAEL D. CHRISTENSEN

We need to set both short-term and long-term goals in our lives. Let me give you an example. When I taught at Viewmont High School in Bountiful, Utah, the basketball team had a goal of taking the state championship. The team had come awfully close the year before and thought they had a good chance of taking state this year. I taught a lot of the players on the team, and their hopes were running high! Though they were shooting for the state title, they realized that they could not achieve that goal unless they achieved the smaller goal of winning individual games. A goal was set to win each game, a small step toward their overall goal. Of course, there is a lot more to achieving a dream or goal than just winning.

Every time they would begin a game, they would huddle up and say something. I couldn't exactly make out what they were saying, so one day I asked a member of the team what they were saying. He made me promise I wouldn't make fun of them! I promised. He told me that every time they broke the huddle, they said, "Love!" "Love?" I questioned. "What does that mean?" He explained to me that the most important goal they had set was not the state championship but to love and support one another no matter what the score of the game. It did not surprise me at all when they ended up winning the state championship that year. Small steps lead to bigger ones, which eventually lead us to the goal of our journey!

How Do You Tackle Your Work?

EDGAR A. GUEST

How do you tackle your work each day?
  Are you scared of the job you find?
Do you grapple the task that comes your way
  With a confident, easy mind?
Do you stand right up to the work ahead
  Or fearfully pause to view it?
Do you start to toil with a sense of dread
  Or feel that you're going to do it?

You can do as much as you think you can
  But you'll never accomplish more;
If you're afraid of yourself, young man,
  There's little for you in store.
For failure comes from the inside first,
  It's there if we only knew it,
And you can win, though you face the worst,
  If you feel that you're going to do it.

Success! It's found in the soul of you,
  And not in the realm of luck!
The world will furnish the work to do,
  But you must provide the pluck.
You can do whatever you think you can,
  It's all in the way you view it.
It's all in the start that you make, young man:
  You must feel that you're going to do it.

How do you tackle your work each day?
    With confidence clear, or dread?
What to yourself do you stop and say
    When a new task lies ahead?
What is the thought that is in your mind?
    Is fear ever running through it?
If so, just tackle the next you find
    By thinking you're going to do it.

$\mathscr{B}$anana Legs

SARA LEE GIBB

$\mathbf{A}$s a young dancer I studied with a distinguished teacher in California, Rozelle Frey. She had been a member of the Anna Pavlova Dance Company in her youth. Her story and influence had remarkable lessons and impact for me. Initially she had trained to become a concert pianist, but when she was taken to see a classical ballet concert, she knew immediately what she wanted to do with her life. There, in her native Sweden, her family, having means, took her to study with a great ballet master teacher. After looking at her work in her audition, he told her that she should continue her career in her piano work, that she had little hope of becoming a dancer. She had a problem that in those days was called "banana legs." Her legs curved outward like bananas. This simply was not compatible with the turnout or rotation of the legs required in the positions of ballet. She pleaded with this teacher to give her a chance to study, to prove herself. She was told that his time was simply too important to work with students who had no potential. However, she could come to the classes, stand back by the piano, and satisfy herself, but she would receive no help or criticism from him and would be completely on her own. She accepted with great enthusiasm.

This was before the time of seriously practiced physical therapy, so the result was unexpected. For seven years she worked diligently—pulling, strengthening, stretching, working. At first she went unnoticed, and then gradually she was accepted into the class and finally placed as an example at the front of the class where the students had to pass the teacher's review.

Through the continued, repeated effort of working the

muscles correctly and placing on them certain demands, the body responded by adapting to those demands. Because she was young and some of the bone was not yet solidified but cartilaginous, her legs became straight and tall. Remember I said she became a member of the Anna Pavlova Dance Company eventually. That is remarkable in itself; but even more startling to me was the fact that of the group of dancers she trained with for seven years, she was the only one who was ever chosen to dance in a professional company. Why? Perhaps the others did not have to try as hard or care so much. We all have stumbling blocks placed in our way—those are our growth-promoting experiences. If ever there was a stumbling block for a dancer, it was banana legs. But she made those stumbling blocks into stepping-stones. They caused her to have to try harder, to be more committed. So Miss Frey rose above those in the ordinary, easier paths, and she was able to reach greater heights.

$\mathscr{A}$ Determination to Succeed

WAYNE B. LYNN

Whereas we cannot control whether we inherit certain aptitudes, we can control our attitudes. A positive approach can compensate for what we may lack in natural ability, especially if we also recognize genuine limitations and concentrate on our best skills.

I remember a student who had a great desire to be the kicker on his high school football team. His first attempts at kicking were almost comical. He could kick the ball only a short distance, with little or no control. The ball was as likely to land out-of-bounds as on the playing field. That he had no natural aptitude for this skill was abundantly clear. What he did have, however, was an unusual determination to succeed.

He continued to practice faithfully. Long after other players had showered and gone home, he was still on the field working on his kicking. Other players steered clear of him to avoid being enlisted to return his punts as he tried again and again. He also took time to watch videos and to carefully study the techniques of successful professional players. He talked to coaches. He became acquainted with college players who kicked for their teams, and he learned from them.

His kicking improved dramatically. His efforts eventually earned him not only the position as the kicker on the high school team, but an athletic scholarship to attend his state university. He played as the kicker on the college varsity team. Later he helped train other aspiring youth in acquiring this skill.

On the other hand I vividly remember a schoolmate who had an unusual aptitude for kicking. Kicking came to him so naturally that, with very little coaching or practice, he was selected for the kicker's position on our high school team. That was as far as he went, however, even though he was courted by university talent scouts. His attitude defeated him. He was not willing to pay the price of disciplined practice, so he forfeited not only a position on a team but an opportunity for a college education.

Time and time again I have watched persons with average ability achieve great things because their attitudes were right. When a task is begun with an attitude of succeeding and with enthusiasm, many obstacles can be overcome. The spirit in which we approach a task, or life in general, gives direction to our lives. With the correct attitudes we can raise our sights and multiply our accomplishments. We can achieve things beyond what we thought possible.

$\mathscr{T}$he One-Hundred-Dollar Threshold

STEPHEN JASON HALL

After I was released from the hospital following the diving accident that left me paralyzed from the chest down, for the first few months I was without the aid of a power-drive wheelchair. This was OK as long as I was on hard surfaces like wood or tile or linoleum. But if you put me on carpet of any height or texture, I was dead in the water. One particular autumn day, the builders who were redoing our home to make its facilities accessible to me were getting the final measurements for my bathroom. I went in to make sure that the sink, shower, and toilet would all be the right height for me. I loved to be in the bathroom because of its tile floors, so I was pushing all over the place. I went over to the sink and then to the toilet, then over to the shower and back to the sink, just burnin' up that ol' tile floor; a regular speed demon.

When the measurements were all taken down, Dad waved the checkered flag, signaling that it was time to go, and I headed toward the bathroom door. As I reached the portal I felt a sudden jerk that threw me and my wheelchair back into the confines of the bathroom. Baffled by this unexpected opposition, I looked down to see what gigantic boulder, rolled automobile, or dead body had halted my forward progression. My investigation ended with some pretty disappointing results, for the only possible culprit I could see was a little tiny gold threshold about one quarter of a centimeter high, almost flush with the carpet. I could not believe that such a small obstacle had halted the greatest speedster that bathroom tile had ever known.

Knowing how the incident frustrated me, and loving a challenge as he does, my dad took a twenty out of his wallet and laid it on the floor. That was all the motivation I needed. I was fifteen years old—I'd sell my sister for twenty bucks. Summoning every bit of strength I had, I pushed with all my might toward the evil doorway. Upon my arrival the previous result was repeated, and I was thrown back into the bathroom. Another twenty went on the ground. Again I tried, and again I was unsuccessful. Another twenty. Again I strenuously pushed, and again I was foiled. Another twenty. This continued until there were five twenties on the ground—*one hundred dollars!* Over and over I tried, grunting and sweating, giving everything I had, but to no avail; always I found myself in what had become the depressing confines of my new tiled-floor bathroom.

Seeing that I had lost this battle in the war, my dad picked up the money, came over to me, put his arm around me, looked me lovingly in the eyes, put the bills back in his pocket, and encouraged me to keep trying. In the end that advice has proved to be of more worth to me than piles of twenties. I kept trying, every day for the next month getting my brothers and sister to put me in the bathroom so that I might fight my way out. Finally, thirty days after my first attempt, my front wheels passed the threshold and my back wheels followed. I had overcome! My arms flew in the air as if I were an Olympic champion. I *felt* like a champion. There was no crowd chanting my name and no national press to take my picture for their front page. The hundred dollars was long gone and spent. But all this didn't matter. I had persisted and conquered, and the joy of it was sweet. It was the best one hundred dollars I never spent.

$\mathcal{T}$he Lord's Success Formula

SEAN COVEY

What's wrong with you? Where's the Sean Covey I once knew in high school?" My quarterback coach glared at me in disgust. "Do you even want to be out there?"

I was shocked. "Yes, of course," I stammered.

"Well, to me you look like you're just going through the motions and your heart's not in the game. And if you're not careful"—he spoke gravely—"the younger quarterbacks are going to pass you up and you're never going to play here."

It was my sophomore year at BYU, during the middle of another hot fall football camp. I knew something was amiss when Coach asked me to meet him in the football office after practice. But I had no idea his words would be so jolting.

Eighteen months before this confrontation I had returned home from my mission in South Africa with a dream and a challenge before me. The dream: to become the starting quarterback for BYU. The challenge: to get my now-flabby body back in shape. I set a goal to become the starter in my sophomore year. Another goal was to become an all-American. Weights, passing drills, and whole-wheat spaghetti became my daily routine. Every ounce of my 170-pound frame thirsted for that starting position, or so I thought at the time.

Four of us were competing for the top job that year. Imagine my embarrassment when I learned at the close of spring camp that I was fourth string on the depth chart. The coaches also decided to redshirt me, which meant I could practice but couldn't play in the games. That's like dating a girl for over a year and never even getting a single kiss. Still I continued my intense four-hour-a-day workout sessions in preparation for my sophomore season. I was determined to secure that starting position somehow.

I thought I had been playing well in my sophomore year—that is, until this confrontation. Coach's accusation that I was just going through the motions deeply affected me, not because he bawled me out, and not because he was disappointed in me, but because deep down in my heart—down below all the hard work I prided myself in doing, down below everything I said about wanting to become the starting quarterback—I knew he was right. It hit me like a revelation: even though I was killing myself physically, somehow I had not completely given my heart and mind to the goal. And the discipline of the heart and mind is a much higher discipline than that of the body.

At home that night I sprawled out upon our hard kitchen table, against Mom's wishes, rehearsing his pointed words: "If you're not careful you're never going to play here." How true those words rang! I realized that without a wholehearted and resolute commitment I would never play. Over the next few days I measured my internal reserves to see if I had sufficient resolve to make that kind of commitment. I also considered quitting. After all, in addition to full-time schoolwork, football would take thousands of hours over the next three years, and unless I was truly committed, body and soul, it wasn't worth my time.

"The real tragedy," said President Kimball quoting Arnold Bennett, "is the tragedy of the man who never in his life braces himself for his one supreme effort, who never stretches to his full capacity, never stands up to his full stature" (*The Miracle of Forgiveness* [Salt Lake City: Bookcraft, 1969], p. 94). I've never enjoyed tragedy. So I welcomed President Kimball's challenge and decided to brace myself for a three-year-long supreme effort.

To rise to this higher level of commitment I knew I would need a new strategic game plan that would draw upon the powers of heaven. I don't believe our Heavenly Father cares about football itself, yet I do know that he is interested in our character growth, and if football can provide that, then the Lord is interested in football. This kind of connection may have been part of what the Lord meant when he said, "All things unto me are spiritual" (D&C 29:34).

Over the next several days I found and developed my game plan. I drew the philosophy of it from a scripture found in D&C 90:24. It might be bold of me, but I call this scripture the Lord's success formula. It reads, "Search diligently, pray always, and be believing, and all things shall work together for your good." In this scripture the Lord promises all of us that if we will search diligently (which to me means work hard), pray consistently, and believe, all things—including football or whatever our interest might be—will work together for our good.

It seemed simple. All I had to do was work, pray, and believe, and the Lord would take care of everything else. Did this mean that if I did my part the Lord would make me the starter? Of course not. The Lord cares just as much for other quarterbacks as he does for me. The promise says that all things will work together for my good. Maybe it was for my good to become the starting quarterback, or maybe it was for my good to be a bench-warmer. I didn't know. But I did know that the Lord knew, and I had faith that if I did my part, he would do his—he would magnify my football abilities.

So I began working, praying, and believing. I began setting specific goals, not monthly or weekly, but practice by practice. After practice I lifted weights, ran sprints, threw balls, and watched game films. I tried to develop a friendship with my horselike, 275-pound offensive lineman. In short, I did all I could to *work* diligently. At the same time I made a sincere effort to develop and maintain a closer relationship with my Heavenly Father through *prayer* and to involve him thoroughly in my game plan.

Most important, I *believed*. For me this was the hard part; but this was also the key. This was what I had been lacking before. As Joseph Smith taught, believing or exercising faith requires mental exertion, mental sweat; it requires the discipline of the heart and the mind. I had to learn to put my faith in the Lord's way of doing things and in the Lord's formula for success rather than in my way of thinking and in my way to success.

My game plan began paying immediate dividends. By the end of fall camp I became the sole owner of second string.

The 1987 season began. Games passed one by one—Pittsburgh, Texas—and I saw no action. My arm hung limp after these games because I had warmed up all game long. After all, what if I got in?

At times I was struck with the discouraging realization that, despite all my effort, I might never play quarterback for BYU, as our starter still had another year. That frightened me, especially considering the hundreds of hours I was sacrificing for football. But I recognized that worrying about things outside of my control was faithless. I was using my way of thinking, my arm of flesh. So each time I felt discouraged, each time I found myself worrying about how well the other quarterbacks were playing or what the coaches were thinking, I exerted myself mentally and exercised faith in the Lord's way of thinking: work, pray, believe, and focus on that which you can control—yourself. And when I did this I felt at peace.

Ever so slowly, I kept improving. Things which once seemed impossible for me became easy. Let me illustrate specifically. I have a small hand and never had confidence throwing a fully inflated football. This was no problem in high school because I threw deflated footballs. But in college everyone uses fat, fully inflated balls. Moreover, college refs inflate the balls to the size of watermelons. After returning from my mission I decided to throw a narrower brand of football in practice, different from the lardo brand the varsity used.

But the facts were plain: if I wanted to start, I would have to throw the fatter ball. At the start of fall camp, to my mind effectively throwing that watermelon was absolutely, positively, and in all other ways inconceivable. So I specifically involved the Lord in this problem and set daily goals to conquer it. I put my faith in his way of thinking, not mine. His way states, "All things are possible to him that believeth" (Mark 9:23). In a matter of weeks I was throwing that melon ball better than I had ever thrown a deflated one. To me these results were miraculous. It felt as if I had just won the Heisman Trophy.

In the third game of the season we played the Horned Frogs of Texas Christian on their home field. Early in the game, as in the days of the Mormon pioneers, the sky began raining crickets, blanketing the artificial turf. This proved to be a sign of things to come—our team was being devoured. Since we were so far behind, I sensed that tonight might be the big night, my first chance to play. And like a flock of seagulls I would save the day.

Sure enough, in the third quarter my call came. "Covey," Coach Edwards summoned. "Warm up." I took a big gulp. My heart pounded. My head swam. "This is it!" I thought. "After all these years." I paced up and down the sidelines, envisioning the newspaper headlines the following day—"Covey, in His First Game, Leads Cougars to Comeback Victory."

It didn't turn out that way. We lost the game badly, although I did squish a lot of crickets. I didn't play too poorly, but I didn't set the field on fire either. I was just plain average. And to earn a starting job my playing had to be outstanding, not average. In other words, I felt I got my chance and blew it. After the game it was said that my arm was too weak to ever make it in college football. It was a long plane ride home.

The games continued to roll by—New Mexico, Utah State, Hawaii—and I continued to see little or no action. "Remember the game plan," I told myself. As each game approached I made it my rule to prepare myself as if I were the starter even though I was just a backup. I kept working, praying, and especially believing. And I kept improving. The coaches took notice.

Midseason featured the big game of the year. We played the Air Force Academy, on national television, in Cougar Stadium, in front of sixty-five thousand fans. At the time, Air Force was nationally ranked. And they paraded the best defensive tackle in the nation: a 260-pound, one-man, bench-press-a-million, quarterback-wrecking machine.

The Monday before the big game my quarterback coach (the

same one who had confronted me earlier in the season) called me into his office. By his peculiar manner and tone of voice I knew something was up. "Sean," he said, eyeing me across his desk, "you're our starter for Saturday's game. And you know how badly we need this one." My heart skipped a beat. And as his words sank in, I felt my inner resources convert from six to eight cylinders. To succeed, I would need that additional horsepower. That night, in secret prayer, I thanked my Heavenly Father.

Never have I been as focused on one thing as I was that week. I must have seemed totally spaced out because I didn't hear people when they spoke to me. My mind was elsewhere. It was Beat Air Force or Bust.

Game day was rainy and cold. Before going to eat pregame breakfast with the team, I pulled my warm comforter around my shoulders, glancing at the rain-soaked terrain outside my window. "Seven hours from now we will be victors or defeatees; I will be a hero or a bum," I thought. The anxiety was awful. Yet deep inside, because I had religiously followed my game plan, I felt prepared and at peace.

The game arrived at last.

At kickoff my mouth was so dry I could barely talk. And after one quarter of play, before we knew what had happened, Air Force had scored twice while we had garnered minus six yards total offense and zero first downs. Though being double-teamed, Mr. Defensive Tackle had spent more time in our backfield than I had. Unless we could generate some offense very quickly, the game was lost.

In these circumstances I recall standing on the sidelines, fighting off the doubts which tried to creep in: "This is much more difficult than I ever imagined." "If I don't hurry and lead the team to a score I'm going to get benched and I'll never play again." But I'd prepared myself for tough moments such as this. I prayed silently, exercised faith in my game plan and in all my preparation, and told my mind to clam up!

From that point on I began to lose all concept of self. The Lord helped me forget that I was playing on national television and in front of sixty-five thousand fans. I even forgot about the defensive tackle machine. I just felt like a little boy playing a fun game of football out in the yard. And things began to click.

We beat Air Force that day 24–13, and somehow I was even named the ESPN "Player of the Game." I had achieved my dream of becoming the starting quarterback and was able to maintain that position for the remainder of that year, and for all of the following year.

After the game my eight-year-old brother said to Dad, "I'm sure glad we won the game."

"Why's that, Joshua?"

"Because now they won't call Sean a bum."

Going from backup to starter proved to be a valuable experience, not because I became the starter but because I discovered the Lord's formula for success in D&C 90:24. I discovered again, as I had so many times before, that the Lord is personally involved in the nitty-gritty details of my life. Even though football is only a game, he cares about football because it is important to football players. And most important, I discovered that if I will work, pray, and believe in the Lord's way of thinking, I can live with confidence and without worry, knowing that all things are working together for my good.

The Lord didn't hand me the starting position. But he did magnify my football abilities far beyond what I thought possible. And thus, when the opportunity arose, I was prepared.

The Apostles of Christ had various day-to-day needs and worries. Apparently they asked the Lord, or were thinking: What shall we drink? What shall we wear? Where shall we sleep? And Jesus answered by saying: "Your heavenly Father knoweth that ye have need of all these things. But seek ye first the kingdom of God . . . and all these things shall be added unto you" (see Matthew 6:31–33).

In like manner, we have daily needs, and worries, and questions: Am I good enough to try out for the baseball team, the debate team, the school play? How can I get this boy or girl to notice me? What should I major in? How can I overcome this weakness of mine? What can I do to become accepted, popular, even successful? Or my question: How can I become a better quarterback? If we remove ourselves from these questions and view them from afar they may seem insignificant, even trivial; but when we own them, when they are ours, they become very important and very real. The Lord recognizes this. He knows that such things are important to us, and he has provided the answer as to how to obtain them.

The answer is always the same: put God first by living his gospel and applying his success formula, and he will magnify you in all that in righteousness is important to you, whatever it may be. This he has promised. He will help you in your athletic endeavors, in your relationships, in your schoolwork, and in all your tough decisions. He will help you overcome seemingly insurmountable mental blocks, your personal, fully inflated footballs. His help may not always be what you want at the time or what your "arm of flesh" thinks is best for you, but it will be what the Lord knows is best for you. And isn't it exhilarating to know that all things are working together for your good!

Truly with the Lord on your side, nothing is impossible. As President Ezra Taft Benson put it: "Men and women who turn their lives over to God will find out that he can make a lot more out of their lives than they can. He will deepen their joys, expand their vision, quicken their minds, strengthen their muscles, lift their spirits, multiply their blessings, increase their opportunities, comfort their souls, raise up friends, and pour out peace. Whoever will lose his life to God will find he has eternal life" ("Jesus Christ—Gifts and Expectations," *New Era,* May 1975, p. 20).

$\mathcal{J}$ources and Permissions

Youth of Zion

"Curses, Foiled Again" by Chris Crowe, from *For the Strength of You* (Salt Lake City: Bookcraft, 1997), pp. 50–53. © Intellectual Reserve, Inc. Used by permission.

"On the Front Lines" by Kathryn Schlendorf, from "But If Not . . . Three Words That Eliminate Compromise," in *Feeling Great, Doing Right, Hanging Tough* (Salt Lake City: Bookcraft, 1991), p. 27. Used by permission.

"Liquid Darkness" by Rand Packer. Previously unpublished.

"At the Top" by John A. Green, from the compilation *The Time of Your Life* (Salt Lake City: Bookcraft, 1977), pp. 19–21. © by Intellectual Reserve, Inc. Previously published in the *New Era* magazine. Used by permission.

"Holding the Standard" by Ardeth G. Kapp, from "Being Friends with Those Who Are Not Latter-day Saints," in *Friends Forever,* ed. Randal A. Wright (Salt Lake City: Bookcraft, 1996), p. 106.

"A Dollar Too Much" by Kathryn Schlendorf, from "Lovest Thou Me? Feed My Lambs," in *Sharing the Light in the Wilderness* (Salt Lake City: Deseret Book Co., 1993), pp. 147–48. Used by permission. Another earlier version of this story is told by Brad Wilcox in his article "Helping Youth Follow the Spirit," *Ensign,* April 1992, pp. 19–20.

"Her Future Children" by Curtis L. Jacobs, from "The Second Coming and You," in *Feeling Great, Doing Right, Hanging Tough* (Salt Lake City: Bookcraft, 1991), pp. 54–55. Used by permission.

"The Toast" by Chris Crowe, from *For the Strength of You* (Salt Lake City: Bookcraft, 1997), p. 6. © Intellectual Reserve, Inc. Used by permission.

Service, Love, and Compassion

"The Angel" by Mark Ellison, from "Getting Along, Getting Even, or Getting Out? Loving When It's Hard to Love," in *Finding the Light in Deep Waters and Dark Times* (Salt Lake City: Bookcraft, 1992), pp. 25–28. Used by permission.

"A Chance to Dance" by Shane Barker, from *Be the Hero of Your Own Life Story* (Salt Lake City: Bookcraft, 1994), pp. 76–77.

"Who Can I Make Happier Today?" by Randall C. Bird, from "Being Friends with Peers at School," in *Friends Forever,* ed. Randal A. Wright (Salt Lake City: Bookcraft, 1996), pp. 53–54.

"A Pick-Me-Up" by Stephen Jason Hall, from "Being Friends in Times of Trouble," in *Friends Forever,* ed. Randal A. Wright (Salt Lake City: Bookcraft, 1996), p. 88.

"'You're Going to L.A.'" by Randal A. Wright, from "Being Friends with Jesus Christ," in *Friends Forever,* ed. Randal A. Wright (Salt Lake City: Bookcraft, 1996), pp. 148–49.

"Nobody Is Not Your Name" by Gary R. Nelson, from "Just Call Me Somebody—Nobody's Not My Name," in *Feeling Great, Doing Right, Hanging Tough* (Salt Lake City: Bookcraft, 1991), pp. 16–18. Used by permission.

"What Would Jesus Do—and Why?" by Michael Weir Allred, from "You Tell on Yourself: What You Are Inside Will Show Up Outside," in *Return with Honor* (Salt Lake City: Bookcraft, 1995), pp. 109–10. Used by permission.

"'My Choice Is You!'" by Mark A. Bybee, from "Is It Falling in Love or Growing in Love?" in *Feeling Great, Doing Right, Hanging Tough* (Salt Lake City: Bookcraft, 1991), pp. 65–66. Used by permission.

"Christmas Package" by Shane Barker, from *Be the Hero of Your Own Life Story* (Salt Lake City: Bookcraft, 1994), p. 75.

"Halloween Santa" by Elaine Cannon, from *Be a Bell Ringer* (Salt Lake City: Bookcraft, 1989), p. 100.

"He Knew What Team He Was On" by Kathryn Schlendorf, from "But If Not . . . Three Words That Eliminate Compromise," in *Feeling Great, Doing Right, Hanging Tough* (Salt Lake City: Bookcraft, 1991), pp. 28–29. Used by permission.

"Only What You Give Away" by Wayne B. Lynn, from *Lessons from Life* (Salt Lake City: Bookcraft, 1987), pp. 82–84.

Friendship and Dating

"One of the Best Friends I Ever Had" by Shane Barker, from *Surviving as a Teenager in a Grown-up's World* (Salt Lake City: Bookcraft, 1993), pp. 69–70.

" 'Who Will Be My Friend?' " by Stephen Jason Hall, from "Being Friends in Times of Trouble," in *Friends Forever,* ed. Randal A. Wright (Salt Lake City: Bookcraft, 1996), pp. 83–87.

"Hanging Out with the Ugly Jumpers" by Lisa H. Olsen, from "Being Friends with Young Men," in *Friends Forever,* ed. Randal A. Wright (Salt Lake City: Bookcraft, 1996), pp. 59–63.

"That's What Friends Are For" by Vickey Pahnke, from "That's What Friends Are For," in *Finding the Light in Deep Waters and Dark Times* (Salt Lake City: Bookcraft, 1992), pp. 1–3. Used by permission.

"The Obligation of Friendship" by Edgar A. Guest, from *A Heap o' Livin'* (Chicago: The Reilly & Britton Co., 1916), p. 162.

"Am I in Love?" by Carlos E. Asay, from *The Road to Somewhere: A Guide for Young Men and Women* (Salt Lake City: Bookcraft, 1994), pp. 109–10.

"Packin' Friends" by Stephen Jason Hall, from "Being Friends in Times of Trouble," in *Friends Forever,* ed. Randal A. Wright (Salt Lake City: Bookcraft, 1996), pp. 88–90.

"Being a Friend First" by Ardeth G. Kapp, from "Being Friends with Those Who Are Not Latter-day Saints," in *Friends Forever,* ed. Randal A. Wright (Salt Lake City: Bookcraft, 1996), pp. 106–7.

"The Making of Friends" by Edgar A. Guest, from *When Day Is Done* (Chicago: The Reilly & Lee Co., 1921), pp. 149–50.

Faith and Prayer

"'You Can't Pray a Lie'" by Brad Wilcox, from *The Super Baruba Success Book for Under-Achievers, Over-Expecters, and Other Ordinary People* (Salt Lake City: Bookcraft, 1979), p. 21.

"Praying for Jack" by Mark A. Bybee, from "Did It Really Happen?" in *Return with Honor* (Salt Lake City: Bookcraft, 1995), pp. 16–17. Used by permission.

"Pat" by Jack R. Christianson, from *What's So Bad About Being Good?* (Salt Lake City: Bookcraft, 1992), pp. 75–83.

"'I Was Thirsty . . .'" by Marion D. Hanks, from *Now and Forever* (Salt Lake City: Bookcraft, 1974), p. 15.

"For a Greater Purpose" by John Cristen Crawford, from the compilation *The Time of Your Life* (Salt Lake City: Bookcraft, 1977), pp. 88–90. © by Intellectual Reserve, Inc. Previously published in the *New Era* magazine. Used by permission.

"Please Help Me Win First Place" by Brad Wilcox, from *The Super Baruba Success Book for Under-Achievers, Over-Expecters, and Other Ordinary People* (Salt Lake City: Bookcraft, 1979), pp. 11–13.

"Someone to Eat Lunch With" by Randall C. Bird, from "Being Friends with Peers at School," in *Friends Forever,* ed. Randal A. Wright (Salt Lake City: Bookcraft, 1996), pp. 49–50.

"Saying Prayers" by Jack R. Christianson, from *Be Strong and of Good Courage* (Salt Lake City: Bookcraft, 1994), pp. 76–77.

"A Blessing for the Station Wagon" by Paula Thomas, from " 'Beauty for Ashes': The Art of Seeing Miracles," in *Finding the Light in Deep Waters and Dark Times* (Salt Lake City: Bookcraft, 1992), pp. 67–68, 70–71. Used by permission.

"A Still Small Voice" by Wayne B. Lynn, from *Lessons from Life* (Salt Lake City: Bookcraft, 1987), pp. 23–30.

Attitude and Self-Worth

"*You* Choose Your Attitude" by Shane Barker, from *Be the Hero of Your Own Life Story* (Salt Lake City: Bookcraft, 1994), pp. 47–48.

"Why Don't You Look at the Sky?" by George D. Durrant, from *Look at the Sky* (Salt Lake City: Bookcraft, 1994), pp. 3–5.

"Rehearsing Success" by Suzanne L. Hansen, from "Win from Within," in *Finding the Light in Deep Waters and Dark Times* (Salt Lake City: Bookcraft, 1992), pp. 19–21. Used by permission.

"They Say" by Val C. Wilcox, from Brad Wilcox, *The Super Baruba Success Book for Under-Achievers, Over-Expecters, and Other Ordinary People* (Salt Lake City: Bookcraft, 1979), pp. 69–70.

"The Eighty Percent" by Barbara Barrington Jones, from "Making Positive Changes," in *Feeling Great, Doing Right, Hanging Tough* (Salt Lake City: Bookcraft, 1991), pp. 82–85. Used by permission.

"You Can Be a Hero" by Shane Barker, from *Be the Hero of Your Own Life Story* (Salt Lake City: Bookcraft, 1994), pp. 2–4, 5.

"It Couldn't Be Done" by Edgar A. Guest, from *The Path to Home* (Chicago: The Reilly & Lee Co., 1919), p. 37.

"'Just One of Those Things'" by Suzanne L. Hansen, from "Yagottawanna Win," in *Feeling Great, Doing Right, Hanging Tough* (Salt Lake City: Bookcraft, 1991), pp. 110–11. Used by permission.

"May I Have This Dance?" by Brad Wilcox, from *The Super Baruba Success Book for Under-Achievers, Over-Expecters, and Other Ordinary People* (Salt Lake City: Bookcraft, 1979), pp. 64–66.

"'Jesus Loves You'" by Randal A. Wright, from "Being Friends with Jesus Christ," in *Friends Forever,* ed. Randal A. Wright (Salt Lake City: Bookcraft, 1996), pp. 144–45.

"Hands" by Stephen Jason Hall, from "I Will Overcome," in *Finding the Light in Deep Waters and Dark Times* (Salt Lake City: Bookcraft, 1992), pp. 42, 44–45. Used by permission.

Choices

"Why Did I Jump?" by Kieth Merrill, from "Deciding About Decisions," in *The Time of Your Life* (Salt Lake City: Bookcraft, 1977), pp. 3–6. © by Intellectual Reserve, Inc. Previously published in the *New Era* magazine. Used by permission.

"Extra Squeezes of Cheese—and Other Lessons in Honesty" by Richard G. Moore. Previously unpublished.

"How We Live Today" by Jack R. Christianson, from *What's So Bad About Being Good?* (Salt Lake City: Bookcraft, 1992), pp. 120–25.

"'To Every Thing There Is a Season'" by Carlos E. Asay, from *The Road to Somewhere: A Guide for Young Men and Women* (Salt Lake City: Bookcraft, 1994), pp. 95–96.

"Sticks and Stones" by John Bytheway, from "The Damaging Effect of Gossip," in *Finding the Light in Deep Waters and Dark Times* (Salt Lake City: Bookcraft, 1992), pp. 51–52. Used by permission.

"Prom Dress" by Elaine Cannon, from *Not Just Ordinary Young Men and Young Women* (Salt Lake City: Bookcraft, 1991), pp. 9–11.

"Dress and Appearance" by Randall C. Bird, from "The War in Heaven Is Now Being Fought on Earth," in *Finding the Light in Deep Waters and Dark Times* (Salt Lake City: Bookcraft, 1992), pp. 120–21. Used by permission.

"The Happy Slow Thinker" by Edgar A. Guest, from *A Heap o' Livin'* (Chicago: The Reilly & Britton Co., 1916), p. 103.

Testimony and Missionary Work

"A Relationship with God" by A. David Thomas, from "Feeling Great, Doing Right, Hanging Tough, and in the Light," in *Feeling Great, Doing Right, Hanging Tough* (Salt Lake City: Bookcraft, 1991), pp. 6–8. Used by permission.

"They Knew" by Elaine Cannon, from *Not Just Ordinary Young Men and Young Women* (Salt Lake City: Bookcraft, 1991), p. 6.

"How I Know: A Convert's Shoes" by Chris Crowe, from *For the Strength of You* (Salt Lake City: Bookcraft, 1997), pp. 102–5. © Intellectual Reserve, Inc. Used by permission.

"He Wanted a Testimony" by R. Scott Simmons, adapted from the audiotape *The Scriptures: Sleeping Aid or Power Source* (Salt Lake City: Bookcraft, 1997).

"Football and the Book of Mormon" by Jack R. Christianson, from *Be Strong and of Good Courage* (Salt Lake City: Bookcraft, 1994), pp. 97–98.

"Even at McDonald's" by Ardeth G. Kapp, from "Being Friends with Those Who Are Not Latter-day Saints," in *Friends Forever*, ed. Randal A. Wright (Salt Lake City: Bookcraft, 1996), pp. 93–94.

"Don't You Have Anything Better to Do?" by Allan K. Burgess and Max H. Molgard, from *Being a Terrific Teen in Troubled Times* (Salt Lake City: Bookcraft, 1994), pp. 131–32.

"'What Makes You the Way You Are?'" by Elaine Cannon, from *Not Just Ordinary Young Men and Young Women* (Salt Lake City: Bookcraft, 1991), pp. 19–21.

"She Wanted to Follow Heavenly Father's Plan" by Barbara Barrington Jones, from "The Most Important Thing," in *Finding the Light in Deep Waters and Dark Times* (Salt Lake City: Bookcraft, 1992), pp. 11–14, 15–16. Used by permission.

"Let Your Light So Shine" by Chris Crowe, from *For the Strength of You* (Salt Lake City: Bookcraft, 1997), pp. 41–44. © Intellectual Reserve, Inc. Used by permission.

Family

"A Kidney for David" by John Bytheway, from "Being Friends with Your Brothers and Sisters," in *Friends Forever*, ed. Randal A. Wright (Salt Lake City: Bookcraft, 1996), pp. 43–45.

"'Come On, Lou!'" by Jack R. Christianson, from *What's So Bad About Being Good?* (Salt Lake City: Bookcraft, 1992), pp. 89–92.

"I Decided I Had Better Start Hating My Parents" by Brad Wilcox, from "Being Friends with Your Parents," in *Friends Forever*, ed. Randal A. Wright (Salt Lake City: Bookcraft, 1996), pp. 25–26.

"Old Blue and the New Firebird" by R. Scott Simmons, from "Being Friends with Young Women," in *Friends Forever*, ed. Randal A. Wright (Salt Lake City: Bookcraft, 1996), p. 81.

"Please Bring Us Home" by Janna DeVore, *New Era,* February 1999, pp. 26–27. © Intellectual Reserve, Inc. Used by permission.

"Marci's Proposal" by Carlos E. Asay, from *The Road to Somewhere: A Guide for Young Men and Women* (Salt Lake City: Bookcraft, 1994), pp. 90–91.

"Family Loyalty" by Matthew O. Richardson, adapted from the audiotape *Get Off the Bench* (Salt Lake City: Bookcraft, 1997).

"The Stick-Together Families" by Edgar A. Guest, from *Just Folks* (Chicago: The Reilly & Lee Co., 1917), pp. 50–51.

"Learning Positive Lessons from Negative Examples" by Brad Wilcox, from "Being Friends with Your Parents," in *Friends Forever,* ed. Randal A. Wright (Salt Lake City: Bookcraft, 1996), pp. 30–32.

Gospel Lessons

"Motorcycle Helmets, Sisters, and the Holy Ghost" by Todd Murdock, from "Am I Talking to Myself or Is It the Spirit?" in *Return with Honor* (Salt Lake City: Bookcraft, 1995), pp. 115–17. Used by permission.

"The Obstacle Course" by Vickey Pahnke, from "Highway to Heaven: The Scriptures Will Steer You Right," in *Return with Honor* (Salt Lake City: Bookcraft, 1995), pp. 159–60. Used by permission.

"Honoring the Priesthood" by Allan K. Burgess and Max H. Molgard, from *Being a Terrific Teen in Troubled Times* (Salt Lake City: Bookcraft, 1994), pp. 145–47.

"The Power of the Word" by R. Scott Simmons, adapted from the audiotape *The Scriptures: Sleeping Aid or Power Source* (Salt Lake City: Bookcraft, 1997).

"The Key to Spirituality" by Barbara Barrington Jones, from "The Most Important Thing," in *Finding the Light in Deep Waters and Dark*

Times (Salt Lake City: Bookcraft, 1992), pp. 9–10. Used by permission.

"How to Know How to Know" by Chris Crowe, from *For the Strength of You* (Salt Lake City: Bookcraft, 1997), pp. 106–8. © Intellectual Reserve, Inc. Used by permission.

"Quick and Powerful" by R. Scott Simmons, adapted from the audiotape *The Scriptures: Sleeping Aid or Power Source* (Salt Lake City: Bookcraft, 1997).

A Change of Heart

"Broken Arms, Broken Hearts, and Confession" by Brad Wilcox, from "Broken Arms, Broken Hearts, and Confession," in *Finding the Light in Deep Waters and Dark Times* (Salt Lake City: Bookcraft, 1992), pp. 9–10. Used by permission.

"The Prodigal Daughter" by Carlos E. Asay, from *The Road to Somewhere: A Guide for Young Men and Women* (Salt Lake City: Bookcraft, 1994), pp. 120–23.

"Grizzly" by Jack R. Christianson, from *What's So Bad About Being Good?* (Salt Lake City: Bookcraft, 1992), pp. 1–7, 9.

"'I Just Can't Pray'" by R. Scott Simmons, adapted from the audiotape *Draw Near unto Me* (Salt Lake City: Bookcraft, 1997).

"Marissa's Choice" by Elaine Cannon, from *Not Just Ordinary Young Men and Young Women* (Salt Lake City: Bookcraft, 1991), pp. 6–9.

"Of Foolish Ventures" by Wayne B. Lynn, from *Lessons from Life* (Salt Lake City: Bookcraft, 1987), pp. 62–64.

"The Poison of an Unforgiving Spirit" by H. Burke Peterson, from *A Glimpse of Glory* (Salt Lake City: Bookcraft, 1986), pp. 54–55, 56, 58.

Work and Goals

"From Third to First" by Shane Barker, from *Surviving as a Teenager in a Grown-up's World* (Salt Lake City: Bookcraft, 1993), pp. 21–23.

"Not Afraid to Try" by Wayne B. Lynn, from *Dare to Dream* (Salt Lake City: Bookcraft, 1992), pp. 14–16.

"How Far Is Forty-nine Yards?" by Melvin Leavitt, from "How Far Is Forty-nine Yards?" in *The Time of Your Life* (Salt Lake City: Bookcraft, 1977), pp. 37–39, 42. © by Intellectual Reserve, Inc. Previously published in the *New Era* magazine. Used by permission.

"A Beet Field Lesson" by Carlos E. Asay, from *The Road to Somewhere: A Guide for Young Men and Women* (Salt Lake City: Bookcraft, 1994), pp. 1–3.

"The Most Important Goal" by Michael D. Christensen, from *Just Be Yourself—That's Hard Enough!* (Salt Lake City: Bookcraft, 1997), pp. 110–11.

"How Do You Tackle Your Work?" by Edgar A. Guest, from *A Heap o' Livin'* (Chicago: The Reilly & Britton Co., 1916), pp. 62–63.

"Banana Legs" by Sara Lee Gibb, from "Our Mortal Body—a Sacred Gift," in *Brigham Young University 1988–89 Devotional and Fireside Speeches* (Provo, Utah: University Publications, 1989), pp. 137–38.

"A Determination to Succeed" by Wayne B. Lynn, from *Dare to Dream* (Salt Lake City: Bookcraft, 1992), pp. 45–46.

"The One-Hundred-Dollar Threshold" by Stephen Jason Hall, from "I Will Overcome," in *Finding the Light in Deep Waters and Dark Times* (Salt Lake City: Bookcraft, 1992), pp. 46–47. Used by permission.

"The Lord's Success Formula" by Sean Covey, from *Fourth Down and Life to Go: How to Turn Life's Setbacks into Triumphs* (Salt Lake City: Bookcraft, 1990), pp. 1–8, 10.